No Bad Days

"Jeff is amazing—he has taught me a lot about what it means to be happy despite your circumstances. This book is going to change a lot of lives!"

—Brandon Turner, bestselling author
of *The Book on Rental Property Investing*

Jeff Holst is truly inspirational, a positive thinker who is knowledgeable and insightful as well as entrepreneurial. Whatever he's on, I want some of it.

—Dr. Ian Pearson, futurist

Jeff's story beautifully depicts what it means to be human. His life's adventure will take you from laughter to tears, from inspiration to curiosity, and have you reconsidering how you're living your life. Jeffrey Holst is the most interesting man in the world!

—Dr. Jamil Sayegh, life, business,
and relationship coach

Who are the most interesting people you have ever met? For me, Jeff Holst is on the short list. Jeff never (ever) has a bad day. What's up with that? We all have "those" days…but Jeff never (ever) has a bad day. Why? It's a decision he made long ago. Actually, it's more than a decision…but you need to know his backstory to understand. In *No Bad Days: How to Make Every Day Great*, you can read Jeff's backstory and walk with him as his life was transformed. You too can say goodbye to bad days in your life and make every day great!

—Tim Enochs, co-founder of NEWLife Leadership,
New York Times bestselling author of *On the Clock*

"What impresses me most about Jeff is how insightful he can be. He is always asking and, more importantly, seeking answers to the difficult questions we all face."

—**Harry S. Dent Jr.**, economic futurist, bestselling author, and financial expert

"The more I learn about Jeff's life and his infectious positive mindset the more convinced I am that he needs to share his story with the world. I am excited about his book. I know it will be great and very inspiring."

—**Vinney "Mr. Smiles" Chopra**, bestselling author of *Apartment Syndication Made Easy* and *Positivity Brings Profitability*

"Since meeting Jeff Holst I have yet to have a bad day! Yes, he has had that kind of influence on my life, and I'm certain his new book *No Bad Days* will have the same impact on yours."

—**Frank McKinney**, seven-time bestselling author, including *Aspire!*

"I didn't and never will have time to read Jeffrey Holst's book, but I read a couple paragraphs, which made me want to read a couple more paragraphs, and well—I think that's how you end up reading a book. So read a couple paragraphs when you have some hours to spare. You might end up reading a couple more."

—**Comedian T.J. Miller**

NO BAD DAYS

HOW TO MAKE EVERY DAY GREAT

JEFFREY HOLST

NEW YORK

LONDON • NASHVILLE • MELBOURNE • VANCOUVER

No Bad Days

How to Make Every Day Great

Published in New York, New York, by Morgan James Publishing. Morgan James is a trademark of Morgan James, LLC. www.MorganJamesPublishing.com

Proudly distributed by Ingram Publisher Services.

Morgan James BOGO™

A **FREE** ebook edition is available for you or a friend with the purchase of this print book.

_____

CLEARLY SIGN YOUR NAME ABOVE

Instructions to claim your free ebook edition:
1. Visit MorganJamesBOGO.com
2. Sign your name CLEARLY in the space above
3. Complete the form and submit a photo of this entire page
4. You or your friend can download the ebook to your preferred device

ISBN 9781636980003 paperback
ISBN 9781636980010 ebook
Library of Congress Control Number: 2022941496

Cover Design by:
Chris Treccani
www.3dogcreative.net

Interior Design by:
Christopher Kirk
www.GFSstudio.com

Morgan James is a proud partner of Habitat for Humanity Peninsula and Greater Williamsburg. Partners in building since 2006.

Get involved today! Visit MorganJamesPublishing.com/giving-back

For Becky—without her, there is no me.

CONTENTS

INTRODUCTION

This story is a personal one. It's about my life, but it's also about you. It is my hope that, in reading about the adversity I have faced and the steps I have taken to overcome those challenges, you will find inspiration that will help you deal with whatever life throws at you. My life, like your life, has not been perfect. I have made more mistakes than I care to admit—many more than I have included in this book—but I also live, and have lived, an extraordinary life.

Extraordinary is an extraordinary word. At its root it can be broken into two words: *extra* (or beyond) and *ordinary*. My life is not ordinary. I refuse to live an ordinary life. My life is *extra* ordinary. I live a life that is beyond ordinary, and you can too. I have faced incredible challenges, but through them all I have persevered. It is my hope that by reading my story you will see how you too can live an extra ordinary life. There are millions of people living extra ordinary lives, but there are many millions more who do not. To live an extra ordinary life, you don't have to have any special advantages, nor do you need to be famous or rich. You can be ordinary and still live an extra ordinary life. I know this, because I am just an ordinary guy who has made a choice to live an extra ordinary life. I know that if I can do it, you can too.

It doesn't matter what particular characteristics you have—your age, sex, religion, relative wealth—as long as you are still alive, you still have a chance to live the life of your dreams. We only get one shot at living this life, and it's imperative that we get it right.

Far too many people spend their whole lives dreaming of a future that may never come. Far too many people put their heads in the sand; they go to work, pay their bills, buy some stuff, and do it all again the next day. If you want to live an extra ordinary life, you absolutely have to start now. You have to recognize that trading five days of your life for two days off is a bad deal. You have to realize that trading fifty weeks of your life for two weeks off is an even worse deal. You need to ask yourself, *If I had unlimited money, would I still work the job I currently work?* You need to do whatever it takes to craft the life you want. It's not about being rich or doing the things I have chosen to do. Rather, it's about doing the things *you* would do if money wasn't an issue. It's about actively taking control of your life and making the choices necessary to live the life of your dreams (whatever those dreams are for you). We only get one shot to live this life; we owe it to ourselves, our children, and to the rest of the world to live the best versions of each of our lives that we possibly can. I know your life will not be perfect. I know that you will face challenges and suffer defeats. You will face loss and feel sorrow, but it's important to remember that we all face our own challenges and fight our own battles. We can't control everything that happens to us, but we can control how we react to the junk that occurs. Everyone has bad things happen to them, but everyone also has good things that happen to them.

The moment you accept completely that you and only you can take responsibility for everything that happens in your life is the same moment when you are able to gain control of your life and point it in the direction of your dreams. When you are facing your imminent demise, I can guarantee that you will not regret making an effort to live an extra ordinary life.

How will you feel if you don't make that effort? What regrets will you have?

What follows is told, for the most part, in chronological order and is an accurate reflection of my memories. But my memory—like everyone's memory—is fallible. As a result, it's likely I have made some errors in its telling. That being said, I have done my best to accurately portray the past. I have however, in a few places, changed a detail or two to protect the privacy of some of the people involved.

One

THE BEGINNING

Life is too short to have anything but delusional notions about yourself.
—**Gene Simmons**

Looking back at it now, it's hard to understand why I took the Ginsu knife into the bathroom. It was a bright sunny day in the spring of my seventeenth year. I was healthy and I had recently begun going steady with a girl whom I had been crushing on for some time. She and I had our first kiss on a bridge less than a quarter mile from the bathroom in which I stood holding the black plastic handle of the serrated carbon steel blade.

I wasn't exactly a rebellious teenager, I was the kid who waited until everyone else in the house was asleep and qui-

etly snuck downstairs to watch late night television shows—
not the ones favored by fifteen-year-old boys the world round
(although I'm sure I watched those also), but instead I watched
infomercials. I loved the pageantry of it all. My favorites were
Carleton Sheets's "No Down Payment" system, pretty much
anything by Ron Popeil, and the Ginsu knife.

In the two years since that first kiss, I'd been on a handful of dates with other girls, but I kept longing for the cin-
namon taste of the Big Red gum that she had favored. My
teenage brain had convinced me that she and I were destined
to be together. That thought, the certainty with which I felt this
"destiny," is even more foreign now than the feel of the blade
against my wrist.

My parents fought occasionally while I was young, but
they were also fun parents. We grew up in a simple time; my
mother was always there. She took us on nature walks and
taught us to recognize flowers and birds. We had a beautiful
house, and my siblings and I each had our own rooms. My
room, which was just above the kitchen bath which I was destined to enter armed with the only infomercial product I ever
convinced my family to buy, overlooked an inground pool and
had a view of the park that extended our backyard into a childhood dreamland.

My dad worked long hours but also provided us with an
amazing childhood. He was a lawyer who was always starting businesses, some of which failed, but the majority of them
did not. One summer was spent at an ice cream store and a
miniature golf course, another spent at Jellystone Park camp-
ground. When we weren't at one of my parents' businesses, we

were traveling. We had an old cab-over Tioga motorhome and drove that thing north, south, east, and west. Before I turned fifteen, I'd seen the Grand Canyon, Yellowstone, the Atlantic and Pacific oceans, and even the beauty of Banff and Jasper in the Canadian Rockies.

Many times in my youth my friends had expressed jealousy over my parents. I often heard them say things like "I wish my parents were as cool as yours." I pretty much agreed. If I could go back to the simple days of my childhood and change something, I don't think I would.

When I was fifteen, maybe six or eight months before that Big Red–flavored kiss, my parents called a family meeting. It was the first and only family meeting they would ever call. We sat as a group and listened to them both. It was at that meeting that we learned of some serious issues in their relationship. After all these years, the cause of my parents' relationship woes is not relevant. What matters is that we were told that they believed that, while it wouldn't be easy, they would eventually work out their problems and that they would be okay. They told us at that meeting that the only reason they were telling us of their problems was because they wanted us to know that they would, in fact, persevere. I had never once thought my parents would divorce. When they told us that, in spite of everything they were going through, they would work it out, I believed them.

I took it on faith that my parents would work out their differences and that everything would be just fine. I continued to believe in the unshakable strength of their marriage when my dad moved out, when he moved back in, and then when he moved out again. But by the time I drew the Ginsu blade against my skin, I had accepted that my parents' marriage, which would last nearly two more years, was actually over.

As I placed the blade against my left wrist, I thought about the infomercial in which the presenter effortlessly carved through a copper pipe and then was still able to thinly slice a tomato. I can't say why I didn't go through with the deed. I don't know if I was actually suicidal. In fact, I'm pretty sure I wasn't. I do know though that it wasn't some childish cry for attention, because until writing these words so many years later, I don't think that I've ever told anyone about the Ginsu knife—not even my wife. I also don't think that I truly wanted to die. I stopped without drawing a drop of blood and left only a slight red mark on my wrist that faded in a few hours. I didn't want to die, but I knew that I sure wasn't happy.

As I wrote those words, longhand in a spiral notebook over a cup of coffee at the Track's End, a twenty-four hour cafe in Chattanooga, Tennessee, I felt gratitude. I felt relief, and most importantly, I knew it was time to finally tell this story. Within a few hours after scrawling these words, I read them aloud to my wife and then shared them with a close friend and a near stranger. I don't like to think about that day, but I have done so often, because it was on that day I made a decision that altered the course of my life. As I felt the bite of the blade on my wrist, I stopped. I stopped because it hurt. My wrist hurt. My heart hurt. I was mourning the loss of my childhood, the loss of my innocence.

I grew up in the church, and I believed wholly in the sanctity of marriage and of the marital bed. As the blade brightened my arm, my eyes reddened with tears. I felt such loss, such shame. A few weeks prior, I had lost my virginity. At the time, I thought it was okay because the girl and I were destined to be together. I thought that we would marry. But in that bathroom, I knew it wasn't true. I knew that it had been an excuse, and I mourned for a wife that I had not yet met. I have since forgiven myself and been granted forgiveness by God, but as I write these words, I still mourn for my wife.

A few days after I wrote those words, longhand in a spiral notebook, I used voice-to-text to add them to a Google doc, and I shared them with my wife for a second time. After she read this chapter and the couple that follow, we talked about whether we wanted to share these deep personal feelings with the world, with our families, and with our friends. We had this talk over drinks in the bar at Ruth's Chris Steak House. It had been hot for the previous several weeks, and the humidity had finally broken. It was about seventy degrees, and there was a pleasant breeze. We were sitting on the patio, in the receding sunlight, sipping Jim Beam old fashioneds, a happy hour special.

My wife, Becky, had experienced a tough day at work and was preparing for a trip to Michigan to see my ailing grandmother. I had been up to see her the previous week and sensed that our time with her, at ninety-five, was drawing to an end. Over the previous few years, Becky had grown even closer to my grandmother than I was. For two consecutive winters, she had spent two weeks with my grandmother at my dad's place in Florida. They played cards and swam in the condo's outdoor pool. A photo of my grandmother in the water smiling with my wife brings me great joy. Given her frail state, we thought that it was important for Becky to make another trip up to see her.

Becky has always been a little stressed when it comes to traveling on her own. On top of that, one of her managers had just told her that she was moving back to her hometown and would have to quit. Becky is a general manager for a beauty store and has a small staff of managers that report to her. Turnover is relatively rare for her, but when it occurs, it always adds some stress. As I listened to her tell me about her day, I wondered if it was fair of me to write about the time before we met. It was one thing to share this stuff with her, but now I was planning to share it in a much more public fashion. How did she feel about the knife? How did she feel about my impurity? How would she feel when these things became known? I had long since told her about my time with my high school girlfriend, so that revelation had not been a surprise, but how would she feel about me sharing it?

It's rare that I feel any apprehension when talking to my wife. We have a connection that gives me the freedom to be completely myself, but that night at Ruth's Chris, I did feel some anxiety. Then Becky spoke. It seemed as if she were reading my mind. I hadn't yet figured out how to ask her these things. She had just finished reading what I had written. She said, "Both of us have done things which we would rather not have done. We will always have to deal with the consequences of them, but it's okay." Had we not known each other so well, it would have been possible to misunderstand. It would have been easy to think she was talking about the knife or for that matter about the summer when I bore false witness (more on this to come), but I knew and she knew that we were talking about my first serious girlfriend.

In the days following that first sexual experience, my emotional state had been fluctuating wildly. I vacillated between guilt and wanting more. I wish I could say that after that first time, I chose to stop, but I didn't. It would be more than a couple of years before my relationship with my high school girlfriend would be officially over. While I look back at some of that time with her fondly, in retrospect and with the clarity of the time, I can see that after that day in the bathroom it was already done. I see now that I wanted to stay with her not because of love, but instead because of guilt. It's not that I didn't love her; I'm sure that I did. And to some degree, even though I haven't spoken to her in years, I still do today. I don't know how it is for other people when they look back at their high school loves, but for me I choose to remember the good above all else.

In the spring of 2019, I was invited to speak at a real estate investing conference in Oklahoma City. It was there for the first time that I spoke publicly about the day that I walked into, and ultimately out of, that bathroom. I didn't tell them about the knife or how close I came, because I wasn't ready to tell that part of the tale. In truth, as I write this, I'm still not sure that I am ready. I did tell them what happened next, though. I glossed over the sorrow and the feelings of failure by saying, "When I was seventeen, I was depressed. Maybe not clinically depressed, but I wasn't happy."

I went on to tell them that on that day, I had made a choice to have a good day; I chose to move forward and not look back. I told them that they too could choose to have good days. I told them that in the nearly twenty-five years since I made that choice, I can honestly say I'd not had a single bad day.

Let's stop for one second to let that sink in. It's important to my story, but perhaps it's even more important to you. Twenty-five years! Not a single bad day! As you will see later in this book, I've had some setbacks. I've had some challenges along the way. But I haven't let them ruin my days. I chose to give up bad days, and you can too! It hasn't always been easy, but it really hasn't been that hard either.

I don't know exactly how long I was in that room with the knife, but eventually I heard a knock at the door. I quickly hid the knife in the cabinet under the sink and exited the bathroom.

I'm going to stop here and share how it is that I have managed not to have a single bad day in two and a half decades. That first day, as I left that room, it was hard. The guilt and sorrow I felt compounded as I reflected on that knife. I was scared, and I was afraid that I would never be happy again. I was also afraid of what I might do. But I had one newfound advantage: I knew, at a very deep level, that I wanted to live. I did not want to die.

The fear motivated me, but I still wasn't sure what to do. I don't know how or why I did what I did next, but I do know that it worked. A short time after I left the bathroom, I spoke to myself. I said these words aloud: "Today's a good day." The sheer act of saying those words didn't suddenly or magically make the day a good day, but it did make me feel a tiny bit better. And so I said it again, and then again, and then again. Over and over I told myself, "Today is a good day." I deluded myself into believing that that very worst day of my young life was actually a good day.

The next morning as I brushed my teeth, I looked into the mirror and I thought, *Today is a good day.* I forced myself to constantly say it and think it. Every time I looked in a mirror or started my car, I thought, *Today is a good day.* I created dozens or hundreds of triggers, and each time one of those triggers occurred, I said or thought, *Today is a good day.* I kept doing it until I no longer had to make a choice. And then one day, a few months later, when someone asked me how my day was going, I replied without thinking and without planning a response. I spoke the truth of my heart and said, "I never have bad days."

It may be self-delusion, but I don't think it matters. The truth is that I never have bad days.

"I never have bad days."

I've probably said that phrase one thousand times in the years since the first time that I said it. As a result, I've had hundreds of opportunities to share my belief that happiness is a choice.

There are four primary responses that I get when I explain my thoughts on this topic. It seems likely that you will fall into one of these categories too. The first and most common response is some form of disbelief. These people just aren't ready. They assume that I'm just saying that I never have bad days, but that in reality I too, like them, actually have bad days. These people believe that everyone has bad days because they have bad days. They refuse to accept that some people do not.

I can understand this response. It's hard to accept that your happiness is a choice, and that if you're not happy, you are choosing not to be happy. It's hard to accept that it's your fault you aren't happy. It's hard to accept that you are choosing to have bad days. The reality is that you can choose to be happy, and you can choose to give up bad days. So if you find yourself in this category, dig deep and believe me when I say that I really don't have bad days. It really is a choice.

The second response that I get is some form of "it must be nice." These people believe me, but they don't believe that they too can do it. They think that my life is blessed (which it is) and that it's just easier for me than them (it might be, but as you will read, it probably isn't). Regardless, if you find yourself believing that I don't have bad days but thinking that it's not possible for you to give them up, then think about this: you know it's possible for me, and you know that at least one person has made a choice not to have bad days. If I can do it, then why not you? I know you can do it too. It won't be easy, but like I said before, it also won't be that hard. You need to crush the limiting beliefs that are holding you back. Stop right now and say it out loud: "Today is a great day. I never have bad days."

The third response that I get is the one I hope you've experienced. Every so often I run into a person who, like me, has made the choice and can honestly say that they too never have bad days. If you're in this category, share your experience as often as you can. Tell everyone you know that they too can make the choice. My guess is that if this is you, then you probably already do. Happiness is infectious; it's almost impossible not to share it.

Just last night when Becky and I were in a Lyft en route to Ruth's Chris to drink those old fashioneds. When the driver arrived at our house to pick us up, I asked him how he was doing, and he said, "I never have bad days." This man had been a soldier and had watched more than one of his friends die. He was out of work and driving people around to pay his bills. And he told me without my prompting that he never had bad days. If that guy can do it, why not you?

The final (and rarest) response is the reason I tell this story.

Occasionally, for whatever reason, when I tell my tale, it strikes a chord. It's like lightning in a bottle. When it happens, it's spectacular. I've seen a person's life change before my very eyes. It's almost like magic as they accept that they too can choose to give up on the negativity. These people feel at a visceral level that it is possible to give up bad days and to choose to be happy. I've only been lucky enough to see this happen a couple of times, but those times meant so much. It is my sincerest desire that you too choose to give up bad days. I know it's possible. I know you can do it. Think about me. Think about our driver and what he has been through. If I can do it—if he can do it—why not you?

Good and bad stuff happens to everyone every single day. Choose to focus on the good and minimize the bad. This doesn't mean ignoring the bad. It just means dealing with it to whatever extent is necessary and then moving on.

When was the last time that you had a bad day? Was it recently? Was it today? It doesn't matter. All that matters is

what you do now. You can make the choice. You can decide right now. Today's the day. Choose. Say it with me:
"I never have bad days."
"I never have bad days!"

If you are or someone you know may be struggling with suicidal thoughts, you can call the National Suicide Prevention Lifeline at 800-273-TALK (8255) any time of day or night.

REFLECTION QUESTIONS

1. Do you think you too could give up on bad days?
2. How would your life be different if you never have another bad day for as long as you live?
3. What if you try to give up bad days and fail? What if you are only able to give up most bad days but (unlike me) still have a few every once in a while?
4. What if you try to give up bad days but only have one less bad day than you otherwise would have? Would it be worth the effort if it means that you have fewer bad days?
5. Why not give it a try and see what happens? You might just surprise yourself.

Two

FINDING YOUR PASSION

The Moses of Michelangelo is repre-
sented as seated; his body faces forward, his head with its mighty beard
looks to the left, his right foot rests on
the ground, and his left leg is raised so
that only the toes touch the ground. His
right arm links the Tables of the Law
with a portion of his beard; his left arm
lies in his lap.

—Sigmund Freud, "The Moses of
Michelangelo"

Seated in a serious attitude, he rests
with one arm on the tables, and with the

> other holds his long glossy beard, the
> hairs, so difficult to render in sculpture,
> being so soft and downy that it seems
> as if the iron chisel must have become
> a brush.
> —Giorgio Vasari, "Michelangelo BUON-
> AROTTI of Florence, Painter, Sculptor
> and Architect" in *Lives of the Artists*

I am not the first person to become captivated by Michelangelo's *Moses*. Sigmund Freud first saw the *Moses* in 1901 and spent three full weeks studying it in September of 1913. A short time later he anonymously published "The Moses of Michelangelo," in which he, in true Freudian style, dissects in minute detail the various nuances of the piece. He talks at length about the possible meanings of the placement of Moses's hands and assigns meaning to what could be nothing more than trivial details.

Vasari said of Michelangelo's *Moses* that "the hairs, so difficult to render in sculpture" were "so soft and downy that it seems as if the iron chisel must have become a brush." He went on to state that the "Jews of Rome…still go every Saturday in troops to visit and adore it as divine, not a human thing."

My interest in the *Moses* came not from seeing it for the first time like Freud or from a deep appreciation of art like Vasari, but instead from a story. In the spring of 1999, I was finishing the second semester of my third year of a two-year program at Grand Rapids Community College (GRCC). My parents' divorce had finally concluded less than a year before.

My relationship with my Big Red–chewing first love was long over, and she had drifted from my life and would ultimately end up living in Tucson. I was living in, and paying rent on, a 750-square-foot house owned by my grandmother, then in her mid-seventies. I worked third shift at a 7-Eleven, took classes in the morning, and slept in the afternoons. I was happy, and by that point I hadn't had a bad day in nearly four years. However, I lacked direction.

As a child, I had boldly declared I'd run for president in 2016, something my dad's future (and now deceased) business partner, Tom, loved to remind me of when I ultimately ended up in his and my father's employ years later. Tom loved to tell people about his favorite memory of me as a child of maybe ten or twelve years old, walking a parade route, shaking hands and declaring I was running for president. I would explain to whatever adult would listen that I would be running in 2016, once I had reached the constitutionally prescribed minimum age of thirty-five. I'd tell them that I'd turn thirty-five in April 2013, so I'd have to wait for the following election to run. Ultimately, when Donald Trump set his sights on the office, I made the controversial decision to let him have his shot.

In the spring of 1999, as I was finishing my associate degree, and with my potential presidency still in the far future, Donald Trump was finalizing his divorce from Marla Maples and flirting with a run for president as a member of Ross Perot's Reform Party. I was in my third year at community college, not because my grades were bad or because I had taken a light load, but instead because I didn't know what I wanted to do. As I looked out at the myriad of possible life paths, I had no real plans and had no idea what it was I wanted to do next.

I look at it differently now, but I believed then that I needed to make a single choice. I needed to declare to the world and to myself a single path forward. The only problem was that I didn't know what I wanted to do, or what I wanted to be. Another Tom, in another time, would tell me that he looked at life as a series of seasons. He said these words to me as he was taking over my law practice. He had retired to Florida after a number of years as a successful attorney only to lose his entire 401(k) in the real estate bubble that followed his retirement. As I was handing over the keys to my law practice in the late fall of 2010, he was restarting his legal career, starting a new season in his life. As Tom took those keys, I, too, would be in transition, but I'll save that story for just a little longer and will instead return to the story I heard that spring day in 1999.

I believe that there are certain moments in life that matter more than all the rest. Sometimes these moments are predictable and understandable, like when a person first sees their newborn child, or when they walk across the graduation stage. But more often, they are a surprise. Sometimes, as they occur, you know that your life is changing, but just as often their significance becomes clear only in retrospect. The story of Moses is one such moment for me.

Having grown up in the church, I have essentially always been familiar with the story of Moses's life. Moses was born to a Hebrew slave girl during the reign of Pharaoh. He was placed in a basket and floated down the Nile. Ultimately, he was taken into Pharaoh's court and raised by Pharaoh's daughter. If we were to tell Moses's story as a series of moments, we would talk about the burning bush, the Ten Commandments, the ten plagues, and his death looking down at the promised land. But I suspect that if he were to tell his story, there would be other moments, deeply personal moments, that we do not know about and that in their own way altered the course of his life.

When I was sixteen and seventeen, I worked summers for my uncle at a sheet metal factory. One of those summers, I met and befriended the shop foreman's son, who, like me, was doing non-union summer work. Russ was a few years older than I was and finishing up a second year at GRCC. One hot summer day, Russ and I were tasked with moving large field-stones. We picked them up at a foundry and took them via flatbed truck up to my uncle's partner's summer cottage. Once there, we loaded them into wheelbarrows and rolled them down a hill, piling them up so they could be used to build a retaining wall. This project, which lasted several weeks and took more than a half dozen trips, afforded us a merciful break from the dirty monotony of sweeping factory floors. On days when I was stuck sweeping, I'd come home covered in black metal dust that would turn my shower water into an inky gray sludge. For a few short days that summer, I'd return home relatively clean, with a pleasant muscle ache in my back and shoulders that I associated with a healthy workout.

As we worked, we talked about our lives. I told Russ about the Big Red girl and a few other girls that I had crushes on. Russ told me of college and the girls he met there. I went home that first night and dreamed of college and the adventures I'd have. The next morning, Russ told me of his classes and his post-college plans. On the second or third day while en route to the lake, our conversation turned to religion. Russ was agnostic or perhaps an atheist. Up to that point in my life, I don't think I'd ever met someone who didn't believe in God. I was both intrigued and sad to learn of his disbelief. He asked me why I believed and challenged my answers.

For the first time, I was faced with an intelligent nonbeliever. He argued that the root of my faith was not God, but my upbringing. He pointed out that if I were born in a Muslim country, I'd be Muslim, and that if I'd been born a Buddhist country, I'd be Buddhist. I countered by saying I felt a deep personal relationship with God. He seemed to consider this and asked me if I could hear the voice of God, if God spoke to me. I affirmed that I could. And then he said these words: "No I don't mean internally; I mean, have you actually heard him speak?"

God spoke directly and clearly to Moses. God told Moses exactly what to do. From a burning bush, God commanded Moses to go to Egypt and lead the Israelites to the promised land. God continued to speak directly and clearly to Moses throughout his entire life, but God had not spoken to me from a burning bush. God had not handed me down the Law. He had not brightened my face so that when I descended the mountain the onlookers would describe me as glowing, a condition that through a random mistranslation in the Latin Vulgate Bible would cause Michelangelo and many other artists to place the horns of truth upon Moses' head.

In spite of having not heard God's spoken voice, I lied to Russ and told him that I had. With that lie, I ended the conversation. The moment in which I spoke that lie is an intensely personal and private moment that altered the course of my life. I don't know what happened to Russ after that summer, but as I sit here writing these words, I pray that that single false utterance, which I later admitted to him was untrue, has not kept him from the truth of God's love.

That discussion altered the course of my life. It led me down a path that ended in me questioning my own faith. It led me a few months later to lose my virginity. The doubts sown that day would plague me for the next few years as my family dissolved and as my relationship with that first serious girlfriend evaporated. This period of doubt would carry me forward through the summer and deep into my time at GRCC. I didn't ever reject God or salvation, but I did go through periods of significant doubt. The seed that Russ planted had me wondering what I would have believed if I had instead been born in Cairo or Mumbai. What would I believe if I had been born to atheist parents? Ultimately, my faith would pull me through. The doubts that I felt then would recede, but they would also survive. They would survive for nearly another decade and would only finally be completely killed off by a doctor and a phone call in the fall of 2008.

That moment of weakness in which I bore false testimony to Russ will always haunt me. In the years since, I've had a few close friendships with nonbelievers. I regret lying to Russ, but the remorse that I felt and still feel guides me as I bear witness to my nonbelieving friends.

The next day, I told Russ the truth that I'd not heard the actual audible voice of God. After that day, we never again spoke about religion or God. However, we did have many other conversations. One of them would ultimately lead me to the *Moses*. Russ had a favorite history professor, Roger Schlosser. Russ spoke so highly of Schlosser that summer that a few years later, when I ended up at GRCC, I purposely sought out his classes. It was in one of those classes, in the spring of 1999, that I first heard the story of Michelangelo's *Moses*.

Schlosser was a compelling speaker and had a way of making history come alive. Between my second and third year at GRCC, Schlosser had grown a full beard. He claimed he had done so because he had been traveling in Northern Ireland, and that he figured that if he got into too much trouble, it would be easier to change his appearance by shaving than it would by putting on a fake beard. Looking back now, I have no idea how involved he was in the Irish struggle, but I do know that the late 1990s were a turbulent time for the Irish people. In researching this book, I learned that Schlosser founded the Irish Studies program at GRCC, and that he was soon to be inducted into the Michigan Irish American Hall of Fame as part of their class of 2019.

Those days, by the late morning, I was often dragging. The morning when I heard the story of *Moses* was no different. I had worked the night before from 11 p.m. until 7 a.m., and I had one class at 8:30 a.m. and another at 11 a.m. It was about thirty minutes into my 11 a.m. class, as I fought to stay alert, that Schlosser woke me up. He had been describing the influence of Michelangelo, and for the first time I was beginning to appreciate the meaning of what it was to be a Renaissance man. Michelangelo was a painter and a sculptor, but he was also an architect and a poet. I listened as Schlosser described Michelangelo's accomplishments, how he had painted the Sistine Chapel, designed the dome of St. Peter's Basilica, and how he created some of the most famous and influential art of all time. And then Schlosser told the story of Michelangelo's *Moses*.

He paused briefly to get our attention. Then he said, "Michelangelo's very best work is hidden in a small church on a hill above the Colosseum in Rome." Michelangelo was commissioned by Pope Julius II to sculpt a colossal tomb. The tomb of Julius II, which was originally conceived in 1505 and not completed until 1545 on a much smaller scale, would be one of Michelangelo's greatest disappointments. As originally conceived, the tomb was to be a three-level structure with some forty sculptures. Over the years, the scope and scale of the proposed structure was reduced, leaving a mere shadow of what could have been. But as Schlosser told it that day, what remained contained Michelangelo's greatest work.

The historical facts are unclear, and I have subsequently heard other versions of the same story, but while that moment five centuries past may have had a deep personal significance to Michelangelo or perhaps to some other bystander, the moment that I hold deep within me is of the retelling by Herr Schlosser (as we would occasionally call him).

Michelangelo squatted down on his haunches as the covering was pulled back to reveal his latest completed work. The small crowd there that day stared in silence at the gleam coming off of the freshly hewn and polished marble. Michelangelo stared with a quiet intensity, and the crowd began to stir uncomfortably as they waited for the master artist to speak. Finally, after some time passed, one of his students approached the artist. "Master, say something."

Michelangelo appeared dazed and barely acknowledged the interruption, but then suddenly he came to life. From his side he produced a chisel and threw it across the room directly at his sculpture. As the chisel flew through the air, Michelangelo screamed a single word: "Move!"

Michelangelo was so taken by his own work that he expected it to get up and move.

As I listened to Schlosser, something deep inside me moved. I was happy and healthy. I'd given up bad days, but I didn't have a purpose. I didn't have a passion. I didn't feel so deeply about any future path that I thought it would be possible for me to become so lost in my work that I would throw a chisel and scream "Move!"

REFLECTION QUESTIONS

1. What's your passion?
2. Is there something in your life that's so important to you that you literally would go crazy if you couldn't do it or experience it?
3. What would cause you to scream "Move!" and throw a chisel?

4. Are you so passionate about what you do that you would throw that chisel in front of a crowd? In front of the pope or a president? In front of the most important person alive?

Three

PIVOTAL MOMENTS

> Either define the moment or the
> moment will define you.
> **—Walt Whitman**

The first time I heard the story of the *Moses* was one of the more significant moments in my life. I wouldn't recognize this for quite some time. As I walked out of class that day, I wasn't thinking of Moses or Rome—I was thinking of sleep.

I drove home to the two-bedroom rental house that I shared with my high school pal and best friend Tim. Tim and I became friends during the year between eighth and ninth grades when we were on our way to a weekend church mission trip. I had a portable compact disc player and a handful of CDs. He probably was more attracted to the music than the idea of us being friends. At the time, CDs were relatively new, and the idea of a portable player was almost completely foreign. I'd gotten mine, a month or so earlier, as a birthday gift from my parents. My music selection was an eclectic mix of the year's popular music, Christian music, and miscellaneous CDs given to me by my dad's friend and future partner Tom (this was after the parade incident I mentioned earlier, but still well before the days when Tom would relish telling it to truck salespeople and bankers).

Tim and I rode in the rear-facing seat of my family station wagon listening to Billy Joel, Paula Abdul, Janet Jackson, Alan Jackson, Bon Jovi, and Billy Ray Cyrus. A few years later, Tim, another friend, and I would go to what would be my first live concert featuring none other than Bon Jovi. That night at Wings Stadium in Kalamazoo during the "Keep the Faith" tour, Jon Bon Jovi would perform "Blaze of Glory" from his solo album, and the three of us would belt out the words from our balcony seats just off the stage. Partway through that song, Jon stopped singing and let the crowd take over. Just before resuming to sing the chorus, he seemed to point directly at the three of us and say, "That's as good as it gets," implying that the moments Tim and I had spent in the back of the Pontiac station wagon where we first bonded had finally paid off.

The night of the concert, we were in our first year of high school, and none of us could drive. We rode to the show, some forty-five minutes from our hometown, with my mom and Tom. En route, Tom told us stories about how when he was growing up in New York City, he used to watch the then young Jon Bon Jovi perform at clubs in Manhattan.

Years later, in the spring of 2000, another childhood friend, Pete, and I would travel to New York City and watch Bon Jovi play live in Rockefeller Center on *Good Morning America*. That day would be the first time I'd hear "It's My Life," a song that would speak to me in a way that music seldom does. In truth, it's ironic that I'm spending any time talking about music. I've seen and enjoyed a number of live performances, but I've never really felt the deep connection to music that many people describe. These days, I rarely choose to listen to music at all; I listen to podcasts and audiobooks instead. However, as I look back on the important moments in my life, I cannot deny the influence of the arts. Whether it be *Moses* or music, whether it be a movie or a good book, there is no doubt these things have had a profound effect upon me. Interestingly, in his 1913 essay "The Moses of Michelangelo," Sigmund Freud opened with a similar observation:

> I have often observed that the subject matter of works of art has a stronger attraction for me than their formal and technical qualities...I am unable rightly to appreciate many of the methods used and the effects obtained in art...Nevertheless, works of art do exercise a powerful effect on me, especially those of literature and sculpture, less often of painting.

After leaving school on the day Schlosser told us the story of the *Moses*, I went home and slept. When I woke up later that night to work the third shift at 7-Eleven (a place I would work for nearly eight years between the age of eighteen and my second year of law school), my mind kept drifting back to *Moses*. Just as I can't say why certain songs impact me, I can't really say why the story of Michelangelo's passion surrounding his *Moses* had such a significant impact. But I do know that barely twelve hours after first hearing the story, I had resolved to see it.

The next morning, I stopped by the post office and picked up an application for my very first passport. Within a few weeks, passport in hand, I would find myself on a plane to London. My dad's parents were well traveled, and my own parents had been to Europe on their honeymoon, but all of this travel had occurred outside of my awareness. My grandfather had died when I was young, and my grandmother, who had traveled to Europe and the Middle East and had even visited Russia during the Cold War, had never really traveled after her husband's death, other than to spend her winters in Florida. My parents had gone on a few cruises and had taken us kids on numerous domestic trips, but I wasn't really aware of anyone close to me who had traveled abroad. I had one regular coffee customer who, once a year, would go island hopping in the South Pacific, but he rarely spoke to me, and I didn't learn of his travels until years later.

I had filed my taxes a few months prior, and thanks to a scholarship income tax credit, I was to receive nearly $4,000. This amount boggled my twenty-one-year-old mind. Thinking about that amount, which was fifteen or twenty times my normal weekly take-home pay, I felt rich. It was, and would remain, the most money I ever had at one time until years later, when in law school, I flipped a house with my friend Travis. (That deal, my first intentional foray into real estate investing sometime around 2005, netted me a profit of a few thousand dollars on top of the $3,500 I committed from my student loan proceeds, and filled my bank account with $5,800.)

With my tax return cash in hand and soon to be in possession of a fresh new passport, I called 1-800-Priceline. In those days, before the dot-com bubble, Priceline would let you make only a single offer each day via their toll-free number. I recall vividly the disappointment when, that first day, they rejected my offer of $250 for a round-trip ticket from Detroit to London. Strangely, I have no recollection of the feeling I had when, a few days later, they accepted my offer of $325 and I suddenly found myself in possession of a thirty-day round-trip ticket to England.

I should pause here. My motivation to call Priceline had been to see the *Moses*. I could easily have bought a round-trip ticket to Rome, taken a cab to Piazza di San Pietro in Vincoli, and stood in front of the *Moses* within a day of leaving Detroit. Like many choices made in my youth, the motivation behind my flying to the United Kingdom rather than Italy eludes me. When I tell the story, I generally say I desired a quest, an Indiana Jones–like journey, or perhaps something more in line with Mark Twain's wanderings as described in his extremely dry but highly interesting work *The Innocents Abroad*. In that book, which I have yet to finish even after several attempts, Twain describes a chapel decorated with the bones of the Capuchin monks who had tended it for centuries. He writes that there are more than four thousand departed monks spread about the chapel, their bones neatly separated, with legs in one room and skulls in another. With his classic wit, he points out that "there would be stirring times there for a while if the last trump should blow."

In what might have been my dumbest decision ever, I asked a girl named Stephanie to drive me in my car to Detroit and drop me at the airport. I used a fair chunk of my tax return to purchase a backpack and a Eurail pass, and I definitely could not afford to park my car for thirty days in long-term parking. Getting someone to drive me to Detroit and return my car to my house was probably a good idea, but in retrospect, asking Stephanie to do it probably was not. I met Steph while working third shift at 7-Eleven. She would show up drunk and try to convince me to sell her some beer. Since she was not twenty-one and obviously had a fairly severe drinking problem, I was disinclined to do so. In those early days she would cuss at me, plead with me, and sometimes flirt with me, but then after a few failed attempts to convince me to sell her or buy her beer, she would seemingly accept that I wasn't going to do it and stop asking. Later, there were times when she would come in sober. It was those times when she was not drunk that we would spend time smoking cigarettes and talking about our lives.

For the next couple of years, Stephanie and her drinking problem would pop in and out of my life. She would tell me that she loved me one night, and then the next she would call me crying because some other guy didn't love her back. The on-and-off nature of our friendship, love, or whatever the heck it was was tempered somewhat by my continued determination to never have bad days. But it wouldn't be until Becky and I finally got serious in the days following the 9/11 terrorist attacks on the United States that I'd finally break completely from Steph.

Handing your keys to a known alcoholic and telling her that you wouldn't be back for about a month is not really the smartest plan. Fortunately, as far as I know, my car was never used in a nefarious way, and I am happy to report that Stephanie is now more than a decade sober and is a certified alcohol and drug counselor.

On the overnight flight to London, I was too nervous to sleep. I spent the night alternating between reading my guidebook, watching bad movies with a set of earphones that worked only half the time, and drinking the complimentary red wine. Just before we landed, I struck up a conversation with my seatmate, who had managed to sleep almost from the moment we took off until the captain announced our pending descent into Heathrow. By then, I was exhausted, I hadn't slept, I had spilled an entire mini bottle of wine on my shirt, and I smelled like rotten grapes. The young lady, who was Australian, was on her way back to London, where she was taking a gap year. She would be the first (but not the last) person I would meet whose travels would make me embarrassed to admit that I was traveling for "only" a relatively modest thirty days.

When I walked out of Heathrow airport around nine in the morning, I had been awake for nearly thirty-six hours. The sun was shining, I had a pack on my back, and I had a plan. According to my guidebook, there was a decent hostel at Earl's Court, and I could take the Tube directly there from the airport. I had not had a cigarette in over twelve hours, so my first priority as I was walking out the door was to find a place to light up. As I stood there with my pack on my back and smoking a Marlboro Light, I struck up a conversation with a short, red-headed American guy whose pack appeared to be about double the size of mine. I don't recall his name now, but I do remember that he also had just arrived from the United States, and that he was planning on backpacking for the next three months until the end of summer. This marked the second time in less than an hour that I'd been embarrassed at the relative duration of my thirty-day trip.

As it turned out, my new friend was also heading to the hostel at Earl's Court, and so we resolved to find the Tube together. Like me, he was exhausted and just wanted to find his way to a bed. Navigating the transportation system in London is fairly easy, and we soon found ourselves exiting the Underground at Earl's Court. Walking out of the tunnel, I was struck by the sights and sounds of London. I felt as if I were in a movie. There were row houses on both sides of the road, some of which had signs that said "To Let," which made me think of toilets or, as our English friends say, the "water closet." After smoking another cigarette, the two of us begin £wandering around trying to follow the directions in our guidebook. We walked down one street and up the next, and wandered farther and farther as we tried to find the hostel that was described as being right at the exit to the Tube. As we walked, we heard the repeated call of the ticket touts, and we briefly considered paying forty quid for tickets to see Bruce

Springsteen. After walking around for what seemed like hours (but was probably more like thirty minutes), we gave up and walked into a hotel. We were able to get a room with two beds and a shared bathroom down the hall for around £70 (about $50 each), well above my $20-a-day hotel budget.

After checking in, I took the opportunity to take a shower. By the time I got back to the room, my new friend was fast asleep. As I lay in bed, I briefly considered that he might wake up while I was sleeping and steal my pack. I tucked my money belt into the shorts that I was wearing to bed and fell immediately asleep. I'm not sure exactly how long I slept, but when I woke up, the window was cracked open and I could hear the sounds of "Born in the USA" playing in the distance. My red-headed friend was awake, and the two of us stood in the corner of the hotel room staring out of the window, catching the occasional pyrotechnic display over the top of the Earl's Court amphitheater as we listened to the Boss.

The next morning, I said goodbye to my roommate, whom I would never see again. I took the Tube over to the British Museum and spent the morning wandering through the exhibits. At the time, the museum was moving the Rosetta Stone, and it was separated from the public only by a single velvet rope. When no one was looking, I reached over and touched it. This would be my first contact with Egypt, but as it would turn out, it would not be my last.

REFLECTION QUESTIONS

1. Have you ever had a seemingly insignificant moment that has had a profound impact on your life?

2. How do you identify moments as important?
3. Instead of identifying singular important moments, should you instead just try to value every moment of your life?
4. How can you be sure that this moment isn't one of the important moments in your life?
5. How can you make the most of the here and now?
6. How do you make sure that this moment matters?

Four

GAINING PERSPECTIVE

> Broad, wholesome, charitable views of
> men and things can not be acquired by
> vegetating in one little corner of the
> earth all one's lifetime.
> —**Mark Twain,** *The Innocents Abroad*

I spent the first seven or eight days of my European travels bumming my way around southern England. I made my way up to Bath, where one night, over swigs of Scotch, I played Monopoly and Risk for money with fellow travelers in a hostel kitchen. I won one and lost the other, and ended up about £20 ahead. The Scotch—the first I had ever tried—was a donation from a young American couple on their honeymoon. They were due to fly back in two days and had just learned that they were limited as to how much alcohol they could legally bring home. I had only turned twenty-one years old a few months earlier, and really hadn't had much experience with alcohol. Bath would also be the first place that I tried gin. As a result, the city has the distinction of being the place I first tried one of my most favorite and one of my least favorite spirits. To this day, I cannot stand the pine-needle taste of gin.

After Bath, I went to Oxford, where William, an American from Atlanta, was spending the summer in England, and I drank Stellas with an Anglican priest. We got into a spirited argument about the monarchy. The priest argued that there was no difference between the monarchy and the "American royal families." It was the first time that I heard the name George W. Bush, whom the priest insisted was destined to be the next president.

My time in the United Kingdom was magical; it was the first time I had been immersed in a foreign culture. It was exhilarating, but I needed to get to Rome. I was, however, a bit nervous about traveling alone in a place where I didn't speak the language. After more than a week in England, I knew I needed to get moving, so I headed to Dover. To calm my nerves, I decided to go to the top deck of the ferry and smoke a cigarette. I lit it up and watched the white cliffs fade into the distance as I smoked. I was officially en route to Calais, France.

I had intended to go to France a day or so after arriving in London. As I stood there smoking, I listened with some interest as a couple about my age were discussing where they were going next. The girl was arguing that they should go to Brussels, and the guy wanted to head to Paris. My plan was to go to southern Spain and Morocco before cutting back across to Italy and Rome. I still had more than three weeks until I had to use my return ticket, and I was interested in going to Paris as well, so I struck up a conversation with a couple. I quickly learned that they were not a couple and had in fact just met. Kate was planning on Belgium, and Mark's plans were even looser than mine. I don't recall how long Kate was planning on traveling, but I know it was much longer than thirty days. Mark had been in England for about two weeks, and was crossing to France to backpack the continent. He hadn't booked a return ticket and figured he'd be able to travel through the summer and possibly longer. He was flexible enough that he suggested we flip a coin: if heads, we would both go to Belgium with Kate, but if tails, Mark and I would go to Spain. Kate was set on going to Brussels. The flip seemed like a good idea, and I agreed. I was secretly relieved that I wouldn't have to travel on my own for the next few days.

I took a one-pound coin out of my pocket, tossed it into the air, flipped it down onto my hand, and up came the queen. So when the three of us got off the ferry, we walked to the train station and booked our tickets to Belgium. With only a few hours before the train was to leave, we sat down at a cafe on a bright sunny day and smoked cigarettes and drank Coca-Cola out of glass bottles. To this day, whenever I drink a glass bottle of Coke, I think of Mark and Kate and wonder what happened to them. The three of us traveled together for about two days, after which I started getting antsy and wanted to go to southern Spain. I told them of my plans, and Kate said she was going to the Netherlands. Mark chose to come with me. I never saw or heard from Kate again.

Mark and I made our way down to southern Spain. On the way we stopped off in Barcelona, where we saw gothic cathedrals, drank super cheap Don Simon boxed wine, and spent the evenings listening to hippies play music on their guitars. Eventually, we ended up in Gibraltar and Algeciras, Spain. I had chosen to travel to Algeciras because I planned to take the ferry to Morocco.

We found a cheap hotel with marble floors and a dark, cool room. It was a nice respite from the travel, and we spent three days wandering around town. We took a sky car to the top of the Rock of Gibraltar, a British colony at the entrance to the Mediterranean. On the rock there's a colony of Bavarian apes, the last of the nonhuman primates found in Europe. Spanish legend has it that when the apes leave the rock the British will go home. Consequently, the British protect the apes, and they're essentially domesticated. One of the apes jumped onto my shoulder and tried to steal my camera. I have a great photo of Mark with an ape on his shoulder grabbing at his hat.

My plan was to take a day trip to Morocco, a new continent and a new country. This was the first time I'd been out of North America, and I was determined to make the most of it. Mark didn't want to spend the money. The ferry cost about $30, and I was still nervous about traveling on my own. We were at an impasse; he didn't want to go to Morocco, and I did. Each morning I would get up and would walk down to the Lighthouse coffee shop, which was right next to the ferry port, and get myself a cup of coffee. I'd sit there for a while and head back to the hotel and spend the day exploring the town and the surrounding areas with Mark. After a few days of this we got on a train headed toward Italy without ever making it to Morocco or North Africa. These days, when I am making travel decisions, I think about Morocco. That choice, my Morocco moment, serves to motivate me as I make my life decisions. It would have cost me $30 and one day to go to Morocco. Choosing to skip Morocco is a regret, but I also recognize that had I gone that day, I might not have made the same choices since that day. I wouldn't have that choice to motivate me, to push me forward, and to help me make bold decisions.

The Lighthouse was a Christian coffee house situated on the crossroads between Europe and Africa. They believed that they would be able to witness to people like Mark, who was a student at the University of Colorado. Like Russ, he was an atheist. Mark and I talked religion over coffee at the Lighthouse, and I told him about Jesus. I have no idea whatever came of those discussions, but what I didn't do is lie to him. I didn't tell him that I heard the physical voice of the Lord.

Almost every time I am called to witness to nonbelievers, I think of Russ and Mark. I wonder how they are and what they are doing. I also often think of the Lighthouse and wonder if it's still there. I will always remember Raymond and Christian and their mission. I think they were doing the Lord's work. While researching this book, I tried to google the Lighthouse and was not able to find any info about it, so I suspect that it is long gone. If you are reading this and happen to know anything about the Lighthouse, please reach out; I'd love to hear the rest of the story.

Mark and I left southern Spain and headed to Italy. My Eurail pass allowed unlimited train travel on a fixed number of days in a thirty-day period. According to the rules, any overnight journey that left after 9 p.m. counted toward the next calendar day. As it turned out, there was a train leaving slightly after 9 p.m., heading toward Italy. It was not scheduled to arrive in Rome until after midnight the following day. In order to save a travel day on our passes, we decided to stop in Pisa. The train was scheduled to arrive in Pisa at 11:55 p.m. This strategy allowed us to get from southern Spain to central Italy while only using a single travel day.

Mark and I arrived in Pisa late that night and checked into a hostel. We had called ahead to make sure that they would have room for us, and when we arrived at the converted church about a mile outside of the central business district in Pisa, we were dead tired. We spent that first day exploring Pisa and eating pasta by the Leaning Tower. I tried gnocchi for the first time, and ever since, gnocchi have reminded me of the tower. It was a relaxing day after our heavy travel day. I was able to get some laundry done. We cooked dinner in the hostel kitchen and spent the evening flirting with a group of college girls from Arizona.

The next morning we took the train to Florence for the day. There, in the Galleria Academia, we saw Michelangelo's *David*. Then we toured the Uffizi Gallery, where I saw my first Michelangelo painting. Michelangelo's painting of the Holy Family, the *Doni Tondo*, is in a room just across from Botticelli's *Birth of Venus*. The main reason that I had wanted to visit the Uffizi was to see the *Birth of Venus*, but as I walked out of that room and into the next, I found myself captivated. The painting of the Holy Family is so lifelike that it seemed as if it were a sculpture on paper. I had never felt this way about a painting before, and rarely have since. As I stood there, I thought about the *Moses* and of Schlosser's proclamation that it was Michelangelo's best work. Was it possible that any man could make art more powerful than the painting before me?

The day after we returned from Florence, Mark and I decided to take a day trip to Rome. The train ride to Rome was significantly longer. We took the early train and arrived in Rome by ten in the morning. We didn't have our bags, which we had left in the hostel in Pisa, so we immediately headed over to the Vatican and St. Peter's Basilica. There, we saw the Sistine Chapel and the *Pieta* (Michelangelo's excellent sculpture of the dying Christ in the arms of his mother). After leaving the Vatican, we headed to the Parthenon, which houses Raphael's tomb, and then rushed back to the train station just in time to catch our train back to Pisa. I had told Mark about the *Moses* and how important it was to me, but I had told him that I wanted to go there alone. I wanted to conclude my quest the way I had started it. Seeing the *Moses* needed to be a deeply personal experience. I left Rome that day without seeing the sculpture.

Mark and I returned to Pisa and to the hostel in the converted church. We spent our last day together wandering around Pisa. We finished the day by walking to the grocery store, where we bought pasta, pasta sauce, and some white wine with Leonardo da Vinci on the label. Then we walked back to the hostel and prepared a meal for ourselves and a couple of our fellow travelers.

The next day, I said goodbye to Mark and left for Rome. We had traveled together for the past two and a half weeks, but it was time to split up. Mark's plan was to save money by working at a farm in Sicily in exchange for room and board, and my plan was to return to Rome and then to travel back to London by way of Paris. In those days, I did not yet have an email address or a Facebook account, so Mark and I exchanged phone numbers. That day as we said goodbye, I was focused on seeing the *Moses* and my return to Rome. I've often wondered what happened to Mark. I did speak with Mark by phone the next fall. We had a short conversation in which he updated me about the rest of his trip and I told him about mine. After that, we lost touch. I'd love to know what happened to Mark, learn about his life, and see where he is now.

About two hours into the trip to Rome, the train came to a stop in the middle of a field of sunflowers. There were sunflowers in every direction as far as I could see. To this day, this remains one of the most beautiful sights I've ever seen. Had the train not stopped, I don't know if I would have ever even noticed them. After seeing the sunflowers, I resolved to pay more attention to the countryside as it passed by my windows. While we were stopped, I struck up a conversation with an American from Nashville who was traveling with his wife and young daughter. Sid told me about the music business and how much he was enjoying his two weeks traveling with his family. He asked me how long I was traveling. When I told him thirty days, he seemed genuinely jealous. That would be the first and only time during my trip that I felt like I was a real traveler.

Eventually the train began moving, and after a short while we arrived in Rome. I immediately made my way to the Colosseum, which I'd seen briefly two days before with Mark. I wandered through the Forum and saw the jail cell where Paul was in prison. Eventually, I made my way to the back side of the Colosseum and climbed the small hill. As I walked, I thought about Michelangelo and Roger Schlosser.

I approached San Pietro en Vincoli (St. Peter in Chains), and I was disappointed to see that the exterior of the church was covered in scaffolding. The façade was not visible, but I had not come to see the church. I was there to be with *Moses*. There was a souvenir vendor with a small cart trying to sell me postcards as I climbed the steps to the church. I ignored him and pressed forward. Years later, when Becky and I climbed those stairs, a vendor with a small cart would try to sell us post cards as well. The first time, I simply ignored the man, but when Becky and I climbed those stairs, I responded in Spanish and feigned confusion. The vendor, possibly the very same one that I had seen seven years prior, knew instantly what I was up to and said in perfect English, "You're not Spanish. I might have believed German, but you are definitely American."

I stood at the entrance to the small church for a moment, reflecting on the journey that I had taken to get there. I was no longer nervous about traveling alone in Europe. But standing there, I was nervous to see *Moses*. I drew in a deep breath and walked into the cool interior of the church. There is an altar at the center of San Pietro that contains a gold box with some very old chains. The Catholic Church believes that the chains held within that box are the very chains that St. Peter wore when he was released from prison by angels. Not being Catholic, I'm not sure if these are the same chains or not, but they are old, and I think there is a real chance that they actually are the chains of St. Peter.

Looking around the room, I searched for the *Moses*. I didn't see it at first. But then, in a dark recess off to my right, I saw a shadowy sculpture. I walked toward it but was unable to see it clearly in the dark corner of the church.

I had a hard time believing that I'd finally made it. This was the moment that I had planned for, and yet all I could see was a shadowy outline. As I drew near, I realized that for a single coin I could light the *Moses*. In front of the *Moses*, there is what can only be described as a vending machine for light. Dropping a single coin into the slot instantly lights the sculpture. I reached in my pocket and found a coin. I dropped it into the machine. I heard the coin clink, and then there was a click. Suddenly *Moses* was awash in light.

I'd like to say that I was in awe, and that I had never seen anything like it before. In truth, I was disappointed. I had worked up this moment so much in my mind that it really had no chance. The *Moses* really is an impressive sculpture. It may be Michelangelo's best work. It may even be the very best marble sculpture in the world. But that day I was let down. I felt different when I returned with my wife in 2006; then, I would be impressed. But in May 1999, at the end of my quest, I found myself mentally comparing it to the *David*, to the *Holy Family*, and to the Sistine Chapel.

I walked out of the church, sat down on the front steps, and lit up a cigarette. I looked down over the Colosseum and thought about the Forum and of my disappointment with the *Moses*. I was done with community college. I was done with my Indiana Jones–like quest, and I still didn't have a purpose. I still didn't know what I wanted to do with my life. Although I wasn't sure what I wanted to do, I didn't regret this quest. I met some great people. I'd seen some great art, and I'd been exposed to things that I had previously only known of in passing. I learned a good deal about myself. I learned that I could confidently travel the world on my own. I realized that I love to travel and that I love to see antiquities. As I looked down at the Colosseum, I thought to myself, *I don't know what I want to do next, but I do know I want to see some more old stuff.* I broke down and bought a stack of postcards. I sat back down on the steps of San Pietro en Vincoli and decided that I would go see some more old stuff. I'd go to the pyramids, Machu Picchu, and Petra. I wasn't sure when or how I would make those trips happen, but I was determined to do it.

REFLECTION QUESTIONS

1. How do you deal with disappointments?
2. Have you ever thought that something would have a big impact on you, only to be disappointed when you finally accomplished or experienced it?
3. Is it possible that sometimes the things that we get are better than what we expected even though they feel disappointing at the time?

Five

LOVING LIFE

Up in the sky great wonders unfold,
tales of men and women both young
and old.
—Jeffrey Holst, "The Fourth of July"

left Rome and headed back toward London. Mark and I
had traveled through Paris en route to southern Spain, but
we had not taken the time to stop. With about a week left
before I was scheduled to fly home, I stopped in Paris. I was
running low on cash, so I stayed in a shared bedroom hostel
in a seedy neighborhood. I spent the last few days of my thirty-day trip in Paris. I toured the Louvre and saw its impressive
art collection, which includes the *Mona Lisa*, *Winged Vic-
tory*, and Michelangelo's *Dying Slave*. I wandered among the

graves at Père Lachaise Cemetery. I visited the Cathedral of Notre Dame and saw its famous flying buttresses. Becky and I would later return to Paris and see many of these same sites, including the magnificent Notre Dame.

When I arrived back in London a day before I was scheduled to fly home, I was completely broke. I was unsure of where I would stay that night and didn't have any money for food. I had a few minutes left on my phone card, so I called my dad to make sure he would be there to pick me up in Detroit and then on a whim called the only people I knew in London. I had met an Australian couple in a laundromat while in Pisa a few weeks prior. They were both taking a year to work in London and spent their time off touring the continent. Since they were only going to be in Pisa for a few hours and had laundry to do, they asked me if I could watch their clothes while they went to see the Baptistry. They seemed happy to hear from me and invited me to a party they were having later that night. I still had a Tube pass, so I headed over to their flat and ended up well fed and with a safe place to sleep.

Since I still had no idea what I wanted to do, and I had spent all my money in Europe, I decided to take the next year off of school. My friends and family had some serious concerns. We all knew other students who had "taken a year off"—it was essentially code for dropping out. But I wasn't concerned; I always knew that I would go back, and that I would finish. What I didn't know was what I wanted to do. On my year off, I worked at 7-Eleven and Arby's. I smoked a lot of cigarettes and spent inordinate amounts of time and money at Damon's (a sports bar and rib joint), playing trivia and drinking beer with Tim. I wrote poetry and hung out with friends. I took several cross-country road trips, including that trip when Pete and I went to New York to see Bon Jovi.

That next summer, having been off school for twelve months and still not sure what I wanted to do, I decided to enroll at Grand Valley State University. I picked GVSU mainly because it was only a few minutes from my job at 7-Eleven. With no long-term plans in place, I decided to take political science classes, figuring that if I couldn't think of anything else to do, I'd go to law school. In the back of my head, I still thought that I wanted to be the president, and it seemed like as good a strategy as any. It was the fall of 2000—an exciting time to be studying politics. George W. Bush and Al Gore were slugging it out in what would ultimately become the closest election in history. That previous spring, as Bush had worked to secure the nomination, I often thought of that Anglican priest and his claims that the Bushes and the Kennedys were American royalty.

My first year at Grand Valley, I met Jennifer. Jennifer was a tiny girl with a pixie haircut. Jennifer and I had two or three classes together that first semester, and we disagreed on almost every political issue. She supported Gore; I supported Bush. But she was also brilliant and ambitious. She wanted to be a senator, and I wanted to be president. I'd never met anyone like her. We argued constantly, but we also learned to respect each other's intelligence.

As Jennifer and I sparred on the issues, I found myself developing a crush. Every once in a while she would pop into 7-Eleven and hang out for a few minutes. We'd smoke a cigarette or two, and my crush would deepen. One night just after the election, but well before it was decided by the Supreme Court, she showed up to ask me some questions for a school project that she was working on. I answered her questions, and then we started talking about the election. After a while, I noticed her looking over her shoulder and out toward the parking lot. It was then that I realized she hadn't come alone. There was someone in her car. Jennifer told me that she had to get going because her friend, who didn't care for politics, was going to get impatient.

I walked outside with Jennifer and we lit up a cigarette. Becky got out of the car to join us. We were still talking politics, and it was pretty obvious that Becky was annoyed. I wish I could say that it was love at first sight, but it wasn't. I barely noticed Becky, and I don't think I was very nice to her. At that point in my life, I tended to take politics a little bit more seriously than I probably should have. As a result, Becky wasn't particularly impressed with me either. She just wanted to hang out with Jennifer, and here I was, some annoying college friend of hers jabbering about politics. Jennifer and I made plans to meet up at a Steak 'n Shake later that night, and Becky reluctantly agreed to join us. At Steak 'n Shake we smoked cigarettes, drank coffee, and talked about our lives. The next night we did it again. Soon these meetups became a regular thing. Every so often Becky, who was in between jobs, and I would end up there by ourselves.

The election was decided in December with George W. Bush winning by only a few hundred votes. As the Supreme Court announced the results, I was drawn back to Oxford and wondered what it would be like to be drinking with my Anglican friend. Becky, Jennifer, and I hung out often that winter. I moved into my second semester at GVSU and still wasn't sure what it was that I wanted to do with my life.

As the school year progressed, I found myself thinking more and more about my time in Europe and of the decision I had made after first seeing *Moses*. By spring, I decided that it was time for me to go to Egypt. I learned that Grand Valley offered a study abroad option in Cairo, and I leapt at the chance to see the pyramids. Tim and I were still living together, and we would occasionally go to a Chinese buffet just down the street from our house. A few days before I left for my study abroad trip in Egypt, Stephanie, Tim, and I went to that buffet. At the end of the meal, I cracked open a fortune cookie and read my fortune aloud: "You long to see the pyramids of Egypt." I think of that fortune every time I eat Chinese food.

Our group arrived in Cairo in the evening. We had taken a bus from Allendale, Michigan, where Grand Valley was located, to Chicago, and from there we had flown to Istanbul (not Constantinople), where we spent the day touring the magnificent Hagia Sophia and the Greco-Roman museum. We finished our layover in Istanbul with a traditional Turkish meal and shopping in an open-air market. There were seventeen students in our group, plus the professor and his wife. After spending just twelve hours in Istanbul, we headed to the airport and boarded a plane to Cairo.

By the time we arrived it was dark, and we'd been up for close to thirty-six hours. The twelve hours we had spent in Istanbul had been fantastic but exhausting. We were all ready to get to our hotel and check in for the night. After clearing customs and buying our visas, something that you do on arrival in Cairo, we boarded a bus. We were told that the ride to our hotel in downtown Cairo would take about forty minutes. Approximately twenty minutes into the drive, at about 1 a.m., the bus broke down on the side of the highway. Some of my classmates had dozed off while we were driving, but the ones who remained awake appeared to become distraught at our predicament.

I was invigorated. Everywhere I looked there were signs in Arabic. The sights and sounds were unlike anything I'd ever seen. I had backpacked alone around Europe, but while there, you could at least sound out the words on the signs. Looking at Arabic letters all around me, all I saw were squiggly lines and dots. Over the course of the next few days, more than half of the students would break down; the culture shock was too much for them. I never felt that way—I was excited. As other students were crying and begging to be allowed to go home, I was wandering the streets and meeting the locals. One such local, Abdullah, a perfume vendor, would sell me the perfume that Becky would wear on our wedding night. Years later, after I finished law school, I returned to Egypt with my wife and introduced her to Abdullah. After finishing the first draft of this book, I learned that my friend of more than twenty years passed away—another victim of the pandemic sweeping our world. Rest in peace, my friend.

We spent nearly six weeks in Egypt. During the week we would have class; we would study history, Egyptian culture, and Arabic. On the weekends, we would travel to Luxor and

Alexandria. We stopped off in Tanta, Wadi Natrun, and the World War II battlefield at El Alamein.

After three or four weeks in Egypt, we boarded a bus and headed out across the desert. The bus came equipped with an armed guard. The guard carried a fully automatic weapon of some sort and was there to protect us from potential danger as we crossed the mostly empty Sinai peninsula. That first day, we stopped briefly to see the Suez Canal. We weren't allowed to take pictures because the Egyptian government still considered the canal a military secret, and we were lucky that we had a chance to see it at all. (Perhaps the existence of the canal itself is a secret?) It wasn't particularly interesting to look at, but it did mark a significant moment for me. The choice I made with Mark not to go to Morocco still haunted me, at least in part, because it meant that while I had seen the African continent, I had not set foot upon its soil. That issue had been resolved a few weeks prior when I had walked out of the Cairo airport and into the North African city. Unfortunately, while in Istanbul, a city that sits at the bridge between Europe and Asia, I had seen the Asian continent and had not been afforded a chance to visit it. As we crossed the canal, I could credibly claim that I had finally made it to my fourth continent.

From there we continued across the desert to Nuweiba, a resort town on the Red Sea coast just forty or fifty miles south of Israel. That evening we listened to music and sang karaoke under the stars. The next day was spent relaxing. I went snorkeling on a beautiful reef located just off the beach. I saw lionfish, swam with dolphins, and cut my foot on some red coral.

I felt as if my foot was literally in flames. I'd later learn it was probably the appropriately named fire coral.

I swam out about two hundred yards into some deeper water. I was swimming in the Gulf of Aqaba, a narrow band of the sea, and could see the shoreline of Saudi Arabia a dozen or so miles across the water. I stayed out there for some time, thinking about my life and about Saudi Arabia. Then my thoughts turned to southern Spain and a swim I took in the Mediterranean Sea, where I had a similar experience staring across the water at Morocco. To this day, I have yet to set foot in either country.

That night, we went to bed before it was even dark. We got up around 10:00 p.m. and loaded into a bus for the short drive to St. Catherine's monastery at the foot of Mount Sinai. It was dark and cool when we arrived, but the parking lot was full of people. We climbed the mountain taking one step at a time in the dark. Every quarter mile or so, we'd run into a local selling bottled water or snacks. As we walked, we would be passed by tourists on camels, and by locals with camels desperately searching for an out-of-shape American to haul up the mountain. About two hours into the hike, at around 2 or 3 a.m., one such local finally found his mark.

I've always struggled with my weight, and at that time I weighed about 275 pounds. Climbing a mountain in the dark with no landmarks by which to judge my progress was disheartening. With my legs aching and my fat and out-of-shape body revolting, I climbed on to my camel. The camel whined and groaned beneath me. Her trainer and guide apologized as she slowly walked her way up the mountain, saying that she wasn't used to carrying such a heavy load. After feeling bad for the camel for an hour or so, we reached the point some 750 steps below the summit beyond which camels cannot travel. I climbed down and resolved to complete the climb on my own. By that time the sky in the far east was starting to lighten, and I was still not at the top of the mountain. I picked up my pace, determined to make it to the top before sunrise. As the day slowly dawned, I crested the top of the mountain. It was less than thirty minutes before sunrise. I sat down exhausted and leaned against the wall of the chapel that sits on the top of the mountain. The small church marks the spot where God had handed down the Law to Moses.

I was welcomed by several members of my group who were already there and realized that even though I had been convinced I was lagging behind the whole group, there were several people who had not yet made it. There were forty or fifty people on the top of the mountain. Some of them were singing songs. Some of them were praying. But most of them were just sitting in silence, waiting for the sun to break the horizon to the east.

At first I talked about the climb with my Cairo roommate, Joe, but then we too fell into silence. I sat listening to people singing praise songs in the distance and thought about Moses, the Ten Commandments, and the parting of the Red Sea. I thought about how I was sitting on the very spot where God delivered the Ten Commandments to Moses. That it was here that God had spoken aloud to Moses. I still had not heard the voice of God, but sitting there thinking about Moses and about Russ, I could feel His presence.

As the sun rose and illuminated the mountain, people all around me gasped at the view. It looked completely different than I had expected. The mountains were old and rounded off. They were the color of sand. I'd traveled around the desert Southwest United States, but I had never seen anything quite like this. While engaged, Becky and I would later hike in Canyonlands National Park, and I'd be reminded of this scene.

My legs ached as I climbed down the mountain. The climb down was harder than the climb up. By then, the sun was up. It was hot and getting hotter. My thighs burned. We were told to keep moving. It was about ten in the morning when we reached the monastery. St. Catherine's is the traditional home to the burning bush. It also houses an impressive collection of ancient manuscripts, including one of the earliest known copies of the Bible. But what stands out the most to me is the pile of skulls. Like the Capuchin monastery in Rome described by Mark Twain, the monks of St. Catherine's dig up their dead and store their bones aboveground. They don't do this as decoration, like it's done in Rome, but instead out of necessity. There's very little ground in which to bury the dead. And so, when a monk dies, they dig up one of the other monks and take the bones and stack them up and a room over in the corner of the courtyard. We were able to look through a barred window into this room and see a stack of skulls perhaps ten feet by ten feet, and five or six feet tall. I don't know how many skulls were in that pile, but I do know that you never forget the first time you see a stack of skulls.

For Valentine's Day in 2005, I surprised Becky with a spring break trip to Paris and Rome. In Rome, I made a point to check out the Capuchin monastery. There I would see my second stack of skulls and my first chandeliers made out of pelvis and femur bones. Later that day we'd go to San Pietro. While there, Becky and I would drop in a coin and illuminate the *Moses*. I don't recall Becky's reaction to seeing *Moses* that day. But as I looked at it, a half dozen years after I had first seen it, I felt something move.

REFLECTION QUESTIONS

1. Do you feel like something is missing in your life?
2. What are you doing to share your dreams and visions with those who are close to you?
3. Do you know what you want?
4. Have you shared that desire with your friends, family, and loved ones?
5. If you don't share your desires with those people around you, how likely is it that you will ever live the life of your dreams?

Six

CHOOSING TO MOVE FORWARD

He's always chasing after the pot of gold. But when he gets there, at the end of the day, it's just corn flakes.

—Christopher Walken as Morty in _Click_

As I finished up my final year in undergrad, I still wasn't entirely sure what I wanted to do. I was still thinking about law school, primarily as a stalling tactic. The thought was that, since I still wasn't sure what it is I wanted to do with my life, I might as well keep going to school. My relationship with Becky complicated that plan. Becky and I had been spending a lot of time together, and with Jennifer's encouragement, I began dating just after Thanksgiving in 2001. When I came home from Egypt in June 2001, I brought both Becky and Jennifer small vials of perfume made from roses grown on Abdullah's family farm.

On September 11, 2001, I had an early political science class. I was then, and remain now, very conservative. Higher education, particularly political science classes, tends toward the more liberal, even in conservative Western Michigan. In class, we would often get into passionate arguments. These arguments would more often than not carry themselves out into the halls. That day, as we exited the classroom, our conversation was immediately interrupted. We learned that a plane had hit the World Trade Center. One of the professors wheeled a TV into the hall, and just after turning it on, we watched the second plane hit.

I had been through New York one time with my brother, as we were heading to visit a friend in New Jersey, and a second time with Pete when we went to see Bon Jovi on *Good Morning America*. Both times I had seen the towers, but only in passing.

I had an exam scheduled at 9:30 a.m. Still not knowing exactly what was going on, I walked across campus to my class. Just before handing out our exam, the professor stood up and said, "I don't know if you have heard, but there has been a terrorist attack in New York City." Then he passed out our exams. I finished the exam about thirty minutes later and emerged from the classroom into a whole new world. My brother, who was hiking in the upper peninsula of Michigan, wouldn't hear about the attack for another day, and he wouldn't understand the magnitude of it until he emerged from the woods a few days later.

After my exam, I called Becky. She was still sleeping and seemed annoyed that I had awoken her. I told her about the attack and we agreed to meet at 7-Eleven. We were both in shock, and after a few minutes talking with Mike, the owner of the store, we left and went to Damon's to watch the coverage. Damon's was eerily quiet, as everyone there was glued to the screens. We didn't play trivia; we just sat there watching in silence. Sitting alone with Becky barely three months after I had gotten back from the Middle East (and only a few months before we would be officially dating) would be when I first realized how I felt about her. Upon hearing about the attack, I had not tried to reach Jennifer or Stephanie, but instead I had called Becky.

Almost eighteen years later, in April 2019, I would find myself sitting in a bank lobby, watching a live stream of flames engulfing the Cathedral of Notre Dame, and once again I would immediately reach out to Becky. Several years ago, for an anniversary present, Becky gave me a watch on which she had engraved "I still do." I rarely wear that watch any longer, as I prefer the utility of my smart watch (also a gift from Becky), but one thing is certain, as we move into our nineteenth year of marriage: "I still do" as well.

By the spring of 2002, my relationship with Becky was getting more serious, but I wasn't yet ready to get married. I also didn't want to leave for law school and be forced into a long-distance relationship. So I decided to stay at GVSU and pursue a master's degree in business. In between classes,

Becky and I would continue to spend time together, and we would grow even closer. By the fall of that year, I had decided to ask for Becky's hand.

I called Becky's dad and asked him if I could come see him. Becky had instilled in me a healthy fear of her dad, and I wasn't relishing the idea of talking to him one on one. Greg and I are now very close, and I am lucky to have such a great father-in-law, but at the time I had no idea what to expect.

Unsure of how to start, I spent an awkward moment asking him about his day and then I reached into my pocket and pulled out the ring. There are three times that I have seen Greg cry. The first time was that day as I held the ring out to him. The second would be at Greg's neighbor Mary's funeral. I never had a chance to know Mary well; by the time Becky and I were dating, she was already quite elderly. Greg's parents died young, and his sister, herself just barely an adult, became his official guardian. But it had been Mary who had taken over for his parents. Mary and Greg remained close, and she had served as a de facto grandmother for my wife and her siblings. The third time I saw Greg cry would be in my living room on a Saturday night in the fall of 2008.

On our first date, Becky and I had gone to an IMAX movie, and then had gone for burritos at a local Mexican restaurant. The day after I spoke to her dad, I took Becky to an IMAX movie. Afterward, I suggested that we get some burritos, recreating that first date.

As we ate, I thought about the moment. I thought about how to ask her. I fondled the ring box in my pocket. As we were finishing our burritos, Becky told me about a friend from work who had recently gotten engaged at a restaurant, and how embarrassing it must have been. I retracted my hand from my pocket and agreed with her that proposing a restaurant was a terrible idea. It was time for a new plan. Since I had spoken with her dad and had told him what day I would ask her, I knew that I needed to quickly form a new plan.

As we walked out of the restaurant, a light snow began to fall. I had bought her a scarf and a pair of mittens as a Christmas gift and had not yet wrapped them. They were still in a Target bag at my house, the same house I had previously been renting from my grandmother. Becky, who has never been a big fan of snow, shivered as we walked to the car. Seeing this, I told her that I had something for her at my house, only a few minutes away. As we drove to the house, my plan formed in my head. When we got to the house, I ran inside and grabbed the bag.

I exited the house—bag in hand—in time to meet Becky as she came up the front steps. I handed her the bag and said, "I'm sorry that I didn't have time to wrap this. But since it was snowing, I thought you might like these." Becky opened the bag and saw the red and black scarf and mittens. She wrapped the scarf around her neck. She frowned slightly as she placed her hands into the mittens. I had placed the ring still inside of the box into her right mitten. She withdrew the velvet ring box with a puzzled look on her face. My brother was about to be married, and Becky's initial thought was that somehow I had accidentally placed his ring box into her gift. I asked her to open it, and as she did, I dropped to a single knee.

By the summer of 2004, Becky was working for PetSmart and I was still at 7-Eleven. We had been married the summer before, and I was in the process of finishing up my MBA. One day, between classes, I was sitting in a computer lab at the downtown campus, researching the admissions policies for Cooley Law School—one of the worst law schools in the country. I still wasn't positive that I wanted to be a lawyer, and Cooley wasn't my first choice, but it had two distinct advantages: it was local, only eighty or so miles from where we lived, and more importantly, it had the option for a January start. Most law schools at the time only took on students in the fall. It was too late for me to be applying for the fall term, and I didn't really want to take an entire year off. Thus, I was considering Cooley. I had taken the LSAT a few weeks prior, and my score essentially guaranteed me both admission and a scholarship to Cooley.

I felt a tap on my shoulder and turned to see an unfamiliar blond girl. Unsure about who she was, I gave her a puzzled look. She asked me if I had considered Michigan State's law school. I told her that I had, but that I didn't want to take a year off and had decided on Cooley as a result. She asked me about the LSAT and my grades, and then asked me if I had time to talk with some folks at MSU Law.

Less than five minutes later, I found myself speaking to MSU's Connell Alsup, who was a dean in charge of student aid. He asked me about my LSAT score and my educational background. After less than a five-minute conversation, he offered me a full scholarship and a laptop—but only if I could start by August 16.

On my first wedding anniversary six days later, I started classes at MSU. We had not had time to move to East Lansing with the short notice, so I spent the year commuting eighty-three miles each way. The commute had a number of lasting consequences: I gained thirty or forty pounds eating fast food, and I spent an enormous amount of time talking on my cell phone with my friend Jason.

I met Jason in my second year at GVSU. He was a senior in high school, taking college-level political science classes through a dual-enrollment program. By the time I started at MSU Law, he was in his third year at State and was considering law school himself. Since Jason was also living in Grand Rapids, we ended up carpooling a few days a week and became close friends.

The final consequence of the commute was that I lost my scholarship. My scholarship, which was merit-based, required me to maintain a 3.0 grade point average. Law school is graded on a curve. In order to maintain a B average, I needed to be somewhere near the middle of the pack. Most people don't realize that law schools grade on a true curve. Half the students will officially be below average and have the grades to reflect it.

The extra time spent commuting had impacted my grades in two ways. First, I had less time to study, but the second and more significant point of impact was that I didn't realize how much studying my peers were doing. I didn't know about commercial supplements and guides. I didn't know that for every hour in class they were spending another hour or two reading cases—every day.

Our law school exams, which consisted primarily of essay questions, accounted for 100 percent of our semester grades. As I finished my first round of exams, I felt good. I had breezed through my MBA, barely studying; I felt like I had known the answers to the essays that were asked. What I didn't know was that everyone knew the answers, and that just knowing the basics wasn't nearly enough. My first-semester grades came back about three or four weeks into the new semester, and I had piled up a bunch of Cs. I began to seriously worry about my scholarship. At 2.2, my grade point average was far too low. To keep my scholarship, I would have to earn near-perfect grades in the second semester.

The terms of the scholarship required that I maintain the 3.0 at the end of each school year. I finished my 1L year with just over a 2.5 GPA. Since my scholarship covered that first summer session as part of my guaranteed first year, I loaded up on summer classes. I was able to push my GPA a little higher, but I would go into my second year, my 2L year as we called it, without a scholarship.

When my first-semester grades for that first year came back, I briefly considered dropping out, but I resolved to finish. I knew that I wasn't going to be able to save my scholarship, so I mentally prepared myself to take the additional student loans and started the process of sorting out what had gone wrong. Throughout my college career, I had been a solid B+ student. I'd managed to maintain a GPA in the mid-threes at every level in spite of the fact that I rarely studied.

For the first time in my academic career, I felt as if I was failing. In my senior year of high school, I had a number of classes where my grades were less than stellar. But then, I had been distracted; I was working full time and my parents were late in their on-again and off-again divorce. My poor grades had not been a function of me not being able to do the work, but instead were the result of me not caring about it. I had failed to turn in projects and regularly skipped homework. However, whenever I did turn something in, I always received high marks.

As I reflected on what had gone wrong and contemplated whether to continue to pursue a juris doctor degree, it became obvious that if I wanted to regain my scholarship for my third and final year, Becky and I would have to move to East Lansing. Had I been better prepared, it's possible I could have maintained my scholarship despite commuting, but with my GPA still in the mid-twos, I could no longer justify the drive.

Becky was still working for PetSmart and began to research the possibility of a transfer. At the time, PetSmart had one store in Lansing, but as luck would have it, they were in the process of opening a new store not far from campus. When it comes to Becky's career, we have always been blessed with fortuitous timing. Becky was hired as a manager at the new store, and the money and benefits she would receive would make it possible for me to quit working and focus exclusively on turning around my struggling academic career. Had PetSmart not been expanding that year, it would have been much harder (or maybe impossible) for me to focus completely on school. When I was graduating eighteen months later, and we were considering a move back to

Grand Rapids, PetSmart would be in the process of opening a boarding facility and Becky would get another promotion and raise to move back home.

I could have given up. I could have easily decided that law school wasn't for me, but instead I chose to keep going. I chose to persevere. I had already gotten my MBA. I could have "decided" that I wanted to get a job, but that wouldn't have been a choice. It would have been giving up on a dream.

When I was a child, I had no solid plans for my future other than being president, but I thought being a lawyer would be a good fallback. My dad was a lawyer, and it just seemed like the right thing to do. One time, at the age of seven or eight, my mom had taken us to Greenfield Village in Dearborn, Michigan. Greenfield Village is part of the Henry Ford Museum. It is a large outdoor living history museum where actors reenact historical scenes. It has been many years since I have visited the Ford, but I still vividly recall seeing the theater chair in which Lincoln sat when he was shot. I also remember a presentation on Lincoln's life where the speaker asked a group of us kids if any of us knew what lawyers did. I raised my hand and said, "They make money."

In my second year of law school, while still not entirely sure that I wanted to be a lawyer, I was sure about one thing: I wanted to make money. And I knew that if I wanted to do that, I needed to turn my grades around and figure out how to graduate with the lowest amount of student debt that I could. I also learned that if I were to finish my second year with a GPA above 3.0, my scholarship would kick in and pay for my third and final year.

I spoke to my professors. I spoke to fellow students. I researched study methods. Most importantly, I hit the books. I started doing my readings. I purchased study aids and flash cards. The hard work began to pay off; when grades came back for the first semester of my second year, the idea of reinstating my scholarship suddenly seemed possible.

In December 2006, two and a half years after I first set foot on campus at MSU Law, I graduated early and with honors. I had regained my scholarship after my second year. The momentum I had created resulted in me pushing forward toward early graduation. The scholarship that had induced me into law school a semester sooner than I had planned ended up propelling me into graduating a full semester earlier than the majority of my classmates. Since they had paid not only for my first full year including the summer, but also for my final semester, I ended up paying for about 58 percent of my tuition. MSU did not offer a winter start, so the graduating class for the fall of 2006 consisted of only around thirty-five students. These were mainly part-timers, but also a few who, like me, had taken extra classes and were graduating early.

I was selected by my peers to be the graduating class speaker. My whirlwind admission had meant that I had missed orientation. Consequently, I hadn't really understood why, as we approached our first round of exams two years prior, the dean had been hanging posters of a marathon runner all over the law school. I'd later learn that he liked to describe the learning process as a marathon and not a sprint. This description would probably have helped to offset my learning curve and perhaps would have saved my scholarship had I been there to hear it.

As I prepared for graduation, I discussed my upcoming speech with Jeff, one of my law school peers who was also graduating early. He thought that I should talk about the marathon runner. A few days before graduation, en route to my last exam as a law student, I stole one of Dean Alsup's posters. In my speech, I held it up and said to my classmates, "Once we have taken and passed the bar exam, and this guy's job is complete, I ask that you, the graduating class, in honor of this poster, remember the leprechaun. You know, the one from the cereal box—the little guy that is always chasing after the pot of gold at the end of the rainbow."

I went on to explain that we needed to reflect on our priorities; we needed to ask ourselves if we really wanted to work eighty or ninety hours a week so that we could have our name on a door or a sign.

"Remember the leprechaun, because when it's all said and done, and when we finally arrive at the end of the rainbow, it sure would be a shame if all we found was a big bowl of cornflakes."

(The full text of my speech, which was inspired to a large degree by the Adam Sandler movie *Click*, is reprinted in the back of this book.)

Quick postscript on law school: My fellow commuter and now great friend Jason, would go on to law school at the University of Michigan and graduate third in his class. After finishing school, he wrote a book about excelling in law school which was published by Aspen Publishing, the leading publisher of law school textbooks and study aids. My initial struggles, and the strategies I adopted that had allowed me to turn it around, formed the basis for his strategy in law school. I claim no credit for his performance, since Jason is one of the hardest-working people I know, but I am happy that my experience was able to help him excel, and I know that the book he wrote has helped many students since. If by chance you should find yourself considering law school, I highly recommend you check out his book: *Excelling in Law School: A Complete Approach* by Jason C. Miller. He even dedicated the book to me; that being said, I'm not going to dedicate this book to him.

REFLECTION QUESTIONS

1. Have you ever felt like you were failing at something?
2. How do you know when it makes sense to quit? How do you know when to pivot to something else?
3. How can you make sure you aren't making an excuse when you choose to quit?
4. How do you know what's important and what's not?
5. Is it possible that sometimes initial failures lead to your greatest successes?

Seven

FACING LOSS

To give up responsibility for our lives is
not healthy.

—Michael Crichton, *Travels*

The 7-Eleven in which I worked was in Jenison. According to Wikipedia, Jenison is "a census designated place for statistical purposes, but has no legal status as an unincorporated municipality." Jenison is governed by Georgetown Charter Township, which in turn is governed by a board of trustees. In 2008, a few years into my legal career, I would run for and almost get elected to that board. The township offices are situated near the library on Baldwin Street, just behind a large Christian Reformed Church. Baldwin, which is the road that passes for the main street in Jenison, bisects Georgetown Township. The offices, church, and library are at the top of what we as children called Baldwin Hill. At the bottom of that hill is a grocery store and also the 7-Eleven building, now a barbeque joint, where Becky and I met.

Each year, Jenison hosts a Memorial Day Parade. The parade starts at one grocery store near the top of the hill and travels a few miles, ending at the other end of Baldwin in the parking lot of the other major grocery store in town. Three times I have appeared in that parade. The first time was the one in which I announced my pending and now canceled run for the presidency. The second was in high school, aboard a 1951 Dodge fire truck that my dad had bought for my mom purportedly as a birthday gift (my mom was born in 1951, so who knows). The final time was just after I announced my plan to run for trustee. When I look at the photos of me taken on that last trip down the parade route, I'm conflicted. On the one hand, I remember the optimistic feeling that I had that day. My family and several friends had shown up to support my run and we were waving American flags from the back of a pickup truck. But on the other hand, I saw a person who was slowly fading away.

After law school, Becky and I moved back into the small Grand Rapids house in which we had previously lived. At just over seven hundred square feet, the house was about three hundred square feet smaller than the apartment in which we had spent the last eighteen months. In spite of the fact that we had gotten engaged on the front steps of the house, Becky had never really liked living there. Her main objection was the recurring millipede infestation. Our dog, Roxy, and I on the other hand, were happy to be home. As we pulled up to the house, after a year and a half away, Roxy happily ran from the car directly to the front door. We had not been much of a dog family when I was young. Becky, on the other hand, has always loved dogs. When we got Roxy, a few months into our new marriage, she was just six weeks old. Perhaps because she knew that I had not really wanted a dog, she decided that I was to be her person. For the rest of her life, Roxy would be happiest when her nose was snuggled against my neck. Shortly after we got Roxy, I spent an evening assembling a new Weber grill in the living room while Becky was doing dishes in the kitchen. In those days, Roxy, still only a few months old, would constantly disappear. A couple of times, convinced that she had somehow gotten out of the house, we would come back from searching the streets to find her in the middle of our living room floor. One day, I thought it would be funny to hide Roxy, so I set her on top of a small pillow inside of the grill. I turned to Becky and said, "Have you seen Rox?" and then I lifted the cover to the grill and laughingly said, "Look, It's a Rox-a-que."

Becky and I had had great difficulty naming Roxy. She had wanted a girly name, and I was partial to manly names, because I thought it would be funny to have a small female dog named Butch or Brutus. We finally compromised and selected Roxy Balboa. In the end though, she would always be Rox-a-que or Q.

Q and I were inseparable. Even though I had not wanted a dog, I fell completely in love with her. She would follow me around and would jump up and down excitedly whenever I returned home. At night, when I would climb into bed, she would snuggle up by my feet. Often, by the time I would wake up, she would be sleeping next to me with her little head on my pillow. Roxy was a mutt of some sort. When we got her from one of Becky's customers at the pet store, we thought we were getting a Chihuahua, but at twenty pounds she was obviously mixed with something.

Before we returned from Lansing, Becky, who was always a little jealous of how attached Q had become to me, convinced me to get another Chihuahua. We again debated the merits of various names. Finally, in a win for Becky, we settled on Chloe. I was able to get Becky to agree to name her Chloe Sullivan after Allison Mack's character on *Smallville*, a show that I enjoyed at the time (long before Mack's legal troubles). By the time we got our third dog, a Great Dane, in the spring of 2008, I had given up trying to pick names, and Becky chose to call her Stella. Stella lived to be nearly thirteen and a half, making her one of the longest living Great Danes of all time. On her thirteenth birthday, she was even featured on the local news and billed as the oldest Great Dane in America.

After less than a year back in Grand Rapids, the four of us, Becky, Chloe, Q, and I moved to Georgetown Township. The new colonial-style house was just a few miles from where I grew up. After a few years of living away, Becky and I found ourselves living minutes from her parents. The move back home—first to Grand Rapids and then to Hudsonville, the other side of Georgetown Township from Jenison—marked our transition into adulthood.

I was practicing law, and she was managing the PetSmart boarding facility. We had a large house in the suburbs with a pool. We were attending a local church and having regular Sunday dinners with Becky's parents. My dad had quit practicing law at nearly the same time I had gotten admitted to the bar. He had started a trucking company with Tom and decided that after more than thirty years as a lawyer, it was time to focus on business exclusively.

It takes about seven weeks to get the results from the bar exam. Many students spend that period working as a paralegal, but since I was planning to work for my dad, I was able to take some time off. Becky and I decided that it would be a perfect time to go on an adventure. I found cheap tickets to Cairo. Becky had never been to Egypt, and I was excited to show her around.

Before we were married, Becky had barely traveled. Her family had made a few trips to Gulf Shores, Alabama, and one to Gatlinburg, Tennessee. She had also made a few trips to Florida. When we were engaged, we took a trip to New Mexico to see my mother, who was teaching at a small school on a Native American reservation. On that trip, we met up with Bill, a former 7-Eleven customer and friend of mine. Bill, Becky, and I made a quick trip to the Grand Canyon and Las Vegas. It was on that trip to Canyonlands that I would be reminded of Mount Sinai.

After Becky and I got a hotel in Cairo, we spent a few days visiting the pyramids and the Egyptian Museum and reconnecting with some of the people I had met six years earlier in 2001, including Abdullah. We boarded an overnight train to

Aswan. From there we made our way all the way down to the magnificent Temple of Abu Simbel, just a few dozen miles north of Sudan. Abu Simbel has two temples dedicated to Pharaoh Ramses II, likely the Pharaoh of Moses's day. We left Aswan by boat, taking a Nile River cruise to Luxor. On the top deck of the riverboat there was a pool, as is almost always the case in southern Egypt; the days were sweltering hot. We spent our afternoons swimming and reading in the sun. One of those afternoons between excursions to see the temples Komobo and Edfu, while looking at the reeds on the side of the Nile, Becky and I talked about Moses and the extra ordinary story of his life.

From Luxor, we hopped a ride to Hurghada on the Red Sea coast, where we stayed a day in a resort before boarding a ferry to the Sinai peninsula. With several more days before we needed to be back in Cairo to fly home, we decided to take a camel trek to a Bedouin village, where we snorkeled and ate a traditional meal of fresh fish, chicken, and vegetables cooked over a fire. We spent the next day relaxing at a beach bar, where I mentioned to one of the servers that someday I'd like to go to Petra in Jordan. I had wanted to make the trip to Petra ever since that day in Rome when I sat on the steps of the church contemplating my future, but I had not been able to arrange a trip. We were only a few hundred miles from Petra, and its relative proximity was taunting me.

Jordan and Egypt do not share a border. Their borders are separated by a small sliver of Israel. Unfortunately, since we did not have a multiple-entry visa, we would not be allowed to return to Egypt if we left and entered Israel. So even though we were so close, the trip to Petra was impossible. Later that day, as we were walking back to our hotel, I was approached by the owner of the hotel, who also had a small travel agency. Dahab is a small town, and word that I wanted to go to Petra had traveled quickly. Jimmy was convinced that we could take a boat from Egypt, bypassing Israel, and that we could get a special day pass to enter Jordan and see Petra.

The last time I had been in the Sinai, I had gotten up early to make the trek to St. Catherine's and the mountain. This time I would get up early and catch a boat to Asia. In the intervening years, since I had first visited Egypt, I had decided that the peninsula was really a part of North Africa and not a part of Asia. Jordan, however, was without a doubt in Asia. We left Dahab before midnight and didn't arrive at the lost city until just after noon.

The whirlwind nature of the trip meant that we would only have a few hours to see Petra, but it would be enough to walk the mile-long Siq and to see the treasury building. The treasury first came to my attention while I was watching *Indiana Jones and the Last Crusade*. In the movie, Indy discovers a lost city carved into the side of a mountain, inside of which he finds the Holy Grail. The exterior of that city is a real place, and while it does not contain the Holy Grail, the treasury was something of a holy grail for me. I had finally arrived at Petra, the penultimate destination on the short list I created that day in Rome.

The final destination on my personal bucket list was Machu Picchu. In the spring of 2008, as I rode down Baldwin Street waving American flags in my bid to become a trustee, I was planning a trip to Peru to see the lost Incan city of Machu

Picchu. I decided that if I won my election, I would celebrate with a trip to Peru, and that if I lost, I would take the time to distract myself from losing by going to Peru (a win-if-you-win, win-if-you-lose situation). That summer, I bought mailing lists and postcards and made several mailings. I attended board meetings and made public statements about things I thought the board could do better, but for some reason I felt strangely unmotivated to do the door-to-door canvassing I knew would be required to win.

The primary election was on a Tuesday in August. The board was made up of four members, and the top four candidates for each party would face off for the general election in November. I ran as a Republican and came in fifth, just a few hundred votes short. As was always the case in Georgetown Township, all four Republicans easily won their general elections. While there is no way to be sure, I think that had I done the necessary door-to-door canvassing, I would have won that night.

With the election over, Becky and I headed to Peru. We left on a summer morning and arrived in Lima on a winter evening in August. It was our first time in the Southern Hemisphere, and we were excited to be traveling again. Unfortunately, our backpacks, which we had checked in Detroit, did not make the trip, and we were destined to spend our first few days in Lima washing our undergarments in a hotel sink while waiting on our bags.

After our bags arrived, we hopped on a bus to Pisco and spent our fifth anniversary drinking pisco sours with the salty smell of the Pacific Ocean in the air. The next day, we took a boat ride to Islas Ballestas to see the Humboldt penguins and a giant geoglyph. The Paracas Candelabra geoglyph is 595 feet tall and can be seen from more than twelve miles away at sea. It, along with the Nazca lines (only visible from the air), were created sometime between 500 BC and AD 500. The Nazca lines, which are a series of geometric patterns and animal designs, weren't fully described until after the invention of the aircraft.

A few days later, Becky and I hired a pilot to fly us over the lines, and we were amazed to see among the patterns the obviously intentionally designed hummingbird, monkey, and spider glyphs.

From there, we went to Arequipa and then on to Puno and the shores of Lake Titicaca, the highest navigable body of water in the world. Lake Titicaca has a surface elevation of 12,507 feet. On the bus ride over the pass en route to the lake, I became lightheaded and nearly passed out while trying to get to the bathroom at the back of the bus. In Puno, I continued to feel the effects of the altitude and was constantly exhausted. I felt a little better after I took some altitude pills from the local pharmacy, so Becky and I walked over to the town square.

A number of people were milling about in the square, and it appeared that they were setting up for some kind of event. I was still feeling quite fatigued, so I sat down to rest on a stone bench. There was some commotion and suddenly I noticed military vehicles and police cars barricading the roads into and out of the square. Unsure of what was going on, Becky and I started to feel a bit nervous and began looking around for an escape route back to our hotel. With no obvious way out, we had no choice but to stay put. Peruvians, particularly those that live in the high Andes, are fairly short and typically have dark hair. Becky and I, with our blond hair and Western European–sized bodies, were something of a novelty, and I noticed several people (including a few of the soldiers) pointing at us.

A stage was set up at one side of the square, and suddenly a band that I hadn't even known was there began playing the familiar sounds of the "Star-Spangled Banner." I removed my hat, and in one of the most surreal moments of my life, I turned to see an American flag waving over the stage. It turned out the ceremony was to honor an American university that had donated a few dozen wheelchairs to local people.

We left Puno by bus and headed to Cusco, the gateway to Machu Picchu. As we walked around Cusco the next day, Becky and I had a rare fight. She was becoming increasingly frustrated with my laziness. Cusco is a little lower in elevation than Puno, at only just over 11,150 feet, but I was still extremely fatigued. I had become lazier in the previous few years, and my weight had ballooned up to 330 pounds. I had failed to walk in the parade, and instead rode in the back of a pickup truck. I lost the election because I had refused to go door to door. Now, I was resting rather than exploring. She was starting to wonder if her husband had lost his lust for life. On previous trips, I was the one that would drag her from one site to the next, never stopping and always wanting to see one more thing. Now, I was wandering around in a daze and was barely functional.

We left Cusco and headed via train to Aquas Calientes, the town at the foot of Machu Picchu. Aside from Machu Picchu, the village doesn't have much of a draw. Aquas Calientes is named after the natural hot springs that are located at the top of a hill in the town. The locals have converted the natural springs into a series of cascading baths. We got off the train and checked into a hotel. It was still fairly early, and we wouldn't be heading up to the lost city until the next morning. Like most tourist towns the world round, the main square is loaded with souvenir shops, restaurants, and bars catering to tourists. We explored the square, ate some pizza, and had a buy-one-get-one-free drink special. Then we decided to climb the hill to the baths and go for a soak.

As I struggled to climb the hill, I stopped to rest near a local market, where I saw people buying and selling guinea pigs, a local delicacy—one I never did get to try. We soaked for an hour or so and headed back to the hotel relatively early to rest up for our early-morning climb to Machu Picchu.

That next morning, as the bus zigzagged up higher and higher to the start of the short trail up to the Incan city, I was excited. It had been more than nine years since I had first seen the *Moses* and made my short list. I was just about done. The last of that list was just around the next bend. I had not had a bad day in more than twelve years, and still I knew that day would be one of the best days yet.

Machu Picchu sits on the top of a mountain in the Andes, in a region known as the cloud forest. The tree-covered peaks were unlike anything I had seen before. They were exactly how I had imagined them. They were exactly like the photos. We got off the bus, paid an entry fee, and started the climb to the top. The vast majority of the people who visit Machu

Picchu first see it from above. The traditional route, the Incan trail, consists of a strenuous four- or five-day hike ending at the Sun Gate, looking down on the ruins first described by the Yale professor Hiram Bingham III in 1911. These days most visitors approach as we did, first by train and then by bus, but even this approach requires something of a climb. We elected to climb up so that our first view of the city would be from above, a kind of faux Incan trail approach.

Six months or so before we left for Peru, I had quit smoking. But still, as we climbed, I was gasping for breath. I stopped frequently to rest. At one such stop, I said to Becky, "The altitude is really killing me." A passerby jumped in to say, "It's not the altitude; it's the weight."

After what seemed like hours of struggling, we reached the top of the ridge and walked out onto a grassy flat step. Machu Picchu, like many Incan ruins, has a number of agricultural terraces. Behind us, I heard a soft humming sound and turned to see a llama, or perhaps an alpaca. We walked slowly to the edge of the terrace, and before us lay the entirety of the lost Incan village. We posed for photos; I was wearing a black zip-up hoodie and an MSU Law baseball cap. In one photo, I lean over and kiss Becky on the cheek. Clouds block the view behind us, but below you can clearly see the ruins of the city.

After taking some photos, we sat for a break before climbing down to explore the rest of the city. As we sat there, my mind was drawn once again to *Moses* and to that day when I made the list of places I would go. I was literally sitting in the clouds, looking down on the last of my list. Behind me, several alpacas were grazing. I watched the expressions on the faces of fellow travelers as they got their first look at the city. I wondered what it must have been like to be Hiram Bingham and to see this sight for the first time, and I wondered what I would do next. I was thirty years old and had just crossed the last item off my personal bucket list.

While I was still excited about the rest of the trip—we were planning to make a quick stop in the Amazon rainforest—I wasn't sure what I would do next. I had no plans. My campaign had fizzled, and I was settling into the practice of law. On the one hand, I knew that we all needed to settle down at some point. But on the other hand, I didn't want to settle. I wanted to live an extra ordinary life, but I still didn't know what that meant. I still didn't know what I wanted to do.

REFLECTION QUESTIONS

1. What are your dreams?
2. Do you have a list of things you want to do or see?
3. Do you feel like you are settling? Or are you striving for an extra ordinary life?
4. What can you do today to make sure you are moving toward an extra ordinary life?
5. If you finished your goals, what would you do next?
6. Are your goals enough? Are you pushing yourself toward the life of your dreams?

the river's edge. From the bus windows, we watched locals on motorcycles carrying everything from children to fish. The village was vibrant in the exact way I had imagined a remote jungle outpost would be. My heart leapt as we approached a local market, but as soon as we saw it, it was gone. I thought about other places I had seen but had not had a chance to visit. I thought about Jordan and the Dead Sea, which we hadn't had a chance to see in our mad dash to Petra. I thought about Morocco, Israel, and Saudi Arabia– countries I had seen across the water but not visited.

We exited the bus and immediately boarded a small boat, powered by a single outboard motor. The boat resembled a large canoe, with peeling green paint. Unlike a canoe, the boat was covered by a wooden roof, and we were mercifully sheltered from the blazing sun. We traveled with a small group up the "Mother of God" river towards the Bolivian border. As the boat puttered along, we passed gold dredges and small villages with waving children. At one point, the captain pointed to a small island and shouted out over the motor "Isla de los Monos." I nodded, pretending I understood what he was saying.

We arrived at an eco-resort and were greeted with cool drinks. We checked into a cabana-like cabin near the swimming pool. The rest of the evening was ours to explore. Becky and I went for a quick swim in the small pool, had dinner, and retired early for the night. The next morning we took a guided tour of a rainforest trail. We saw giant spiders, and the guide pointed out local plants and insects. He offered us grubs to eat. We passed, but a brave Aussie girl ate one, and when no one else would try the local delicacy, she ate the remaining one. I immediately felt regret that I hadn't tried them, so when the opportunity arose a few minutes later, I ate a termite directly off a tree. Our guide told us that it would taste like mint. It was slightly minty, but in reality the tiny ant-like bug barely had any taste. We visited Isla de los Monos (Monkey Island), where we saw several different types of monkeys, the next day. Later, we went piranha fishing in a creek just off the main waterway.

I didn't catch anything, but I felt a couple of tugs as chunks of rare beef mysteriously disappeared from my line. On the way back to the camp, we went swimming in the river, our guides telling us we had nothing to worry about since the carnivorous fish never swam out in the center of the river; they preferred the banks, where it was more likely a small animal would stop by for a drink. Later that night after dark, we went out on the river and watched the unfamiliar southern stars drift by. After floating a mile or so down the river, the boatman started the engine and turned on some handheld flashlights. The first mate pointed the lights at the shore. We soon were spotting dozens or perhaps hundreds of caimans, a small local crocodile, resting on the banks. We had not seen any during the day as we passed this spot on the way back from fishing. This was likely because they preferred to swim out in the middle of the river where it was possible to grab some tourists cooling off away from the piranha. With our trip to Peru drawing to an end, we headed back to Cusco and then on to Lima.

We had one day in Lima before we needed to head home. We spent the day at the zoo. Becky and I often try to stop at zoos when we travel. Our first such experience was in Cairo in 2007. Just as in Lima, we had found ourselves in Cairo with one day left before our flight home. Abdullah recommended we go to the Giza Zoo. Our only plans upon returning to Cairo from the Sinai had been to get some pizza.

On the last day of my first trip to Giza in 2001, a few of us ate at a Pizza Hut located at the foot of the pyramids. From its upper floors, you can look out the window and see the classic view of the Great Sphinx lined up directly in front of the three pyramids of Giza. That last view of the Giza necropolis had been a great way to end my first time in Egypt, and Becky and I had determined we would repeat it. Since we had the whole day, and the zoo was in Giza, we hopped a cab and headed over.

We were the only tourists at the zoo, and we happily paid the tourist price of about fifty cents. At the time, the locals could get in for about one tenth the price. Almost immediately, it became obvious that this zoo was unlike any we had been to before. Prior to that day, our zoo highlights had been feeding giraffes in Battle Creek and watching giraffes procreate in Chicago. We had always liked zoos and had gone to several when we were dating, but hadn't been to a zoo since I started law school nearly three years before.

Our time at the Giza Zoo set the bar for every zoo I have been to since. The zookeepers took us into the back rooms and cages. They created photo ops for us by handing us animals. In one photo, I am seen holding a juvenile Nile crocodile (much smaller than the caimans of Peru); in another I am posing with small snakes on my head. We have photos of Becky playing a real-life game of Hungry Hungry Hippos and of feeding elephants and giant seals.

It wasn't just the photo ops; it was also the animals. There were all sorts of birds and small mammals that we had never seen anywhere before, and some mammals we had seen many times before but never in a zoo. They had cages with pacing rottweilers and other domestic dogs. These displays were among the most popular, with throngs of children *ooh*ing and *ahh*ing. The only animal the children found more exotic that day was Becky and her blond hair. The children took turns getting their photos taken with the two of us and then with Becky by herself.

We finally broke away from the children and started to head for the exit. En route, we passed a tiger cage. The bars appeared flimsy, and it seemed as if the tiger, who was pacing rapidly back and forth, could have pushed its way through. Just before we were to exit, I felt a tug on my arm, and a middle-aged Egyptian man mumbled something under his breath. I hadn't made out what he said and assumed he was asking for baksheesh, a local combination of tip, bribe, and charity. In Egypt, particularly in the tourist spots, Westerners are subjected to constant requests for baksheesh. I tried to ignore him.

"Wait. Did he say something about a baby lion?" We hadn't seen a baby lion, and so I stopped to listen. He was asking me in broken English if I wanted to pet a baby lion. In exchange for this experience, this one last photo, he wanted a tip of about five dollars, an exorbitant amount of baksheesh by Egyptian standards but well worth it to get a photo with a baby lion. I quickly agreed and handed over a fifty-pound note. He looked around furtively before pocketing the money. He quickly rushed us around a corner and through a nondescript fence. He stopped and again looked around nervously. He was obviously checking to see if anyone was watching. He pulled open a door and hurried us inside. We suddenly found ourselves in a dark room lined with green bars. On the right was a cage that contained a large sleeping lioness. Our guide pointed and said "mama." The bars were about a half-inch thick and had gaps large enough that I could have stuck my hand in and touched the mother lion. We were ushered further into the dark, cavernous room and instructed to wait while the baby was brought out to us.

A moment later, our guide, who may or may not have worked for the zoo, opened a smaller cage on the left and cajoled a "baby" lion, which appeared to be more like a yearling, out into the unprotected area where we stood. It was the size of a large Great Dane, perhaps 150 pounds, and its mane had already begun to grow. Hearing the commotion, the mama lioness woke up and began nervously pacing and grunting at us. The baby sauntered out of his cage and lay down on the floor at our feet. Our "guide" had us straddle the young lion and quickly took our photos. In these photos you can see the look of shock on my face and the look of terror on Becky's. After escaping the lions' den, we left the zoo and ate our pizza.

The Lima Zoo was not at all like the zoo in Cairo. I wandered around in a daze. I was getting a cold and was fatigued. I barely remember that zoo. If it were not for the photos, I don't know if I'd remember it at all. A few days earlier, in Cusco, just before we left for the rainforest, I had received an email from an employee giving me their two-week notice. As I prepared to board the plane home, I was exhausted. Becky and I were still at odds over my laziness, and I was trying to process how to move forward at the law firm. Less than a week before, I had completed my personal bucket list, and now I was beginning to spiral.

We arrived home at the end of summer, and I went to work trying to figure out how to cover my client's cases without the help of a second attorney. A few days after getting home, I could barely get out of bed. I was having trouble breathing and decided to head to a medical center. I told them about my travels, and about an elderly Englishman who had died with a breathing issue while we were at the eco resort. They tested me for TB, which I did not have, and then, without confirming a diagnosis, they prescribed some antibiotics and sent me home to rest. Short an attorney, I didn't have time to rest, so I went to the office instead.

A few days later, on Saturday, September 6, 2008, I returned to the medical center. It was obvious that the antibiotics were not working. I had a couple of swollen bruises that had appeared on my abdomen. This time, they took blood and told me to keep taking the antibiotics. Still unsure of what was causing my illness and thinking I might have picked up something in the Amazon, I was again sent home to rest. I was seriously worried. I was struggling to breathe, my vision was blurring, and the lumpy bruises on my stomach seemed to be hardening. I was tired all the time, and I was near certain that I had picked something up while traveling. My thoughts kept returning to people I had seen over the last few weeks while traveling. An elderly British man died in a remote jungle outlet. Struggling to breathe, he was rushed via a long canoe-like boat upriver to the nearest doctor, some three hours away. Did I have what he had? A middle-aged Peruvian man sat next to me on the plane. He was hacking and blowing his nose the entire flight. An obnoxiously screaming baby rode the bus to Cusco and stopped crying only long enough to cough deep, throaty coughs that often left them gasping for breath. Did any of these people have weird, hard, lumpy bruises? Had I picked something up while swimming?

When Becky got home from work that night, we ate dinner and settled in for a quiet evening of television. A new season of *Heroes* was starting, and we wanted to catch up before it began. Around ten o'clock that evening, Becky's cell phone rang. It was the medical center doctor. He asked for me. My phone was dead, and Becky's dad was our emergency contact. The doctor had called my phone first, and when I didn't answer, had called her dad, who had given him Becky's number. Becky handed the phone to me, and I listened as the doctor said the words that finally killed off the doubts instilled in me by Russ all those years earlier.

In the days before Facebook, I had lost track of Russ and Mark. I still don't know what happened to them, but the doubts I had felt when talking to them had lingered in my mind. I was going to church regularly and even occasionally would have breakfast with our new pastor. My doubts were fading with time as I was settling into a routine, but every so often I'd wonder: *What's the point? How do we know that God is real?*

Why doesn't God make it easy for us? Why doesn't He speak out loud to us or to me like He had to Moses?

The doctor started by saying "There is no easy way to tell you this."

I remember every word he said that day. They are burned into my mind with a clarity unlike any other conversation I have ever had. It was the intensely personal moment that would change everything for me. The doctor continued by saying, "You have leukemia, and you need to go to the hospital immediately."

I heard the words clearly, and I fully understood. I said, "Okay." He said, "Do you understand what I am saying?" And I said, "I do. I need to go to the hospital right now." He asked me which hospital I was going to go to, and I named one downtown. He said that he would call ahead with my records and let them know I was on the way. He repeated again, "It's important you understand: you have to go now."

I hung up. Becky asked me what the doctor had wanted, and I said, "Let's finish this episode of *Heroes*." There were only a few minutes left, but she wasn't having it and was insistent that I tell her what he had said. In that moment, the diagnosis was personal to me, and I knew that it was a moment that would change everything. I wanted just a few more minutes, but I also knew that my wife had a right to know. I said aloud for the first time the same words that I have said so often since: "I have leukemia."

Becky was understandably upset and started to cry. I resolved to get ready to head to the hospital but knew that Becky wouldn't be able to drive. She was simply too upset.

I finally understood why I was getting increasingly lazy and why I was losing my passion to explore. At that moment, I knew why I hadn't campaigned the way I should have and why I had so disappointed my staff attorney that he had decided to quit. I was exhausted, and this knowledge crashed down on me all at once. I instantly knew everything, and in that instant, my exhaustion had multiplied exponentially.

I called Becky's dad and asked him to come over. Becky couldn't calm herself enough to reach out to him. He arrived a few minutes later to see his daughter weeping on the couch. He tried to talk to her, but she was nearly incoherent. For the second time in a half hour I declared, "I have leukemia." This time I added "And I need to go to the hospital." Greg immediately lost it. He collapsed onto the stairs. After a few moments, he regained some of his composure and asked us to pray with him. At that moment, the last of my doubts evaporated. I felt an incredible peace. I knew that no matter what happened next, I would be okay, and that Becky would be okay too.

I still worried about how my wife would react and how she would support herself if I were gone, but I also knew deep inside that it would all be fine. I felt a peace that surpasses understanding. I resolved to focus on the task at hand. My immediate concern was to get my wife into the car for the trip to the hospital. I remember telling her I was going to get a change of underwear and some socks. I told her that I thought there was a chance I'd be staying a few days in the hospital. To this day, it bugs me that I didn't think to bring a book or pair of sweatpants.

We hopped into Greg's vehicle and headed downtown. I still didn't know what my purpose was, but I was content. I had lived well. I had completed my bucket list. I had seen the *Moses*, the pyramids, Petra, and Machu Picchu. I swam with sharks in Belize and drank wine on Jim Morrison's grave. I had married well, and we were happy.

In the car on the way to the hospital, I called my mom and said, "I don't know anything, but I am on the way to the hospital, and I have leukemia. I just thought you should know." And then I called my dad, my brother, my sisters, and a bunch of friends. By the time I arrived at the emergency room, less than an hour after first learning of my fate, I had said those words dozens of times.

Soon people started showing up at the ER. Suddenly my dad and mom, my brother, one of my sisters, and a couple friends were there, all likely thinking I had only called them. When my brother arrived, he was upset, but tried to make light of the situation by calling me out. He said, "I told you that you can't always have good days." I replied by saying, "It's not too bad. I just wish I could have finished *Heroes*."

The thing is, it wasn't a bad day. In many ways, I was dealing with it better than anyone around me. I immediately accepted what was told to me; I never questioned it. And I was okay. I wasn't happy to have a potentially life-ending disease, but I also never considered having a bad day. I was thirty years old, and I had already lived an incredible life. I did not want to die, but I accepted that I might. More than a decade before, I had chosen to live in a world where it wasn't possible to have a bad day, and this day was no different. It was just another good day.

Later that night I'd learn that my white blood cell count was over 250,000. The normal range is between four and eleven thousand. A few years prior, we had lost my cousin Kimberly to leukemia, and I knew that her blood counts had never been this high. It was then that I accepted not that I *might* die, but instead that I *would*. For two days, while we waited for the results of a bone marrow biopsy, I believed that I was on the way out. I believed fully that I had weeks, not months or years, left to live. I wrote a will and living trust and had my assistant, a notary, come to the hospital and sign it with me. I prepared to die.

Those two days were good days. One of my nurses had been my babysitter years before, and I enjoyed seeing her again. My wife stayed by my side for hours every day, and when she would go home at night to rest, I would walk the halls of the hospital and talk with the staff. I accepted my fate and prepared for an uncertain but short future. One day, my dad told me that if I lived until February, less than six months away, he would take me to Australia. I replied without hesitation that my goal was to see Christmas. I wanted to say goodbye and to celebrate one last time.

REFLECTION QUESTIONS

1. Who would you call if you suddenly found out you had a potentially life-ending disease?
2. Have you lived the kind of life that you can be proud of living?

3. What would you do differently if you knew you had only a year to live?
4. Who would you spend your last days with? What would you do?
5. Do you think it's possible to truly give up bad days?
6. Are you ready to live an extra ordinary life? If not, what's holding you back?

Nine

BOTTOM TIME

We live as we dream—alone. While the
dream disappears, the life continues
painfully.

—Joseph Conrad, *Heart of Darkness*

It took more than two years before I would reach rock
bottom. It was one thing to be sick. It was an entirely different thing to fail. A few days after that first night in the
ER, I got good news. The bone marrow biopsy had come back,
and I had chronic myelogenous leukemia (CML). For a lot of
people, this would be bad news, but for me it was like being
surprised with a life sentence when I was certain I would get
the death penalty. I didn't want to die, and now I was being
offered a chance to live.

A few years prior, the prospects for someone diagnosed with CML were bleak, but by the time my entourage arrived at the hospital, my chances were significantly better. In the decades leading up to my diagnosis, the five-year survival rate for CML had hovered between 10 and 20 percent and was much lower if you were in the later stages of the disease. I, however, would benefit from recent scientific advances. I was prescribed imatinib. Imatinib was first approved for medical use in the United States in 2001, and as far as I could tell, it was a miracle drug. It does not work for everyone with CML, but imatinib worked for me. Within a few weeks, my white blood cell counts began to fall dramatically. By my second follow-up, barely a month after finding out about the disease, my white blood cell count had dropped from 258,000 to about 50,000. After four months, it was within the normal range. I continued to see my oncologist monthly for another eighteen months, during which time my white blood cell counts stabilized and the testing revealed a continued reduction in the Philadelphia chromosome.

As I understand it, CML is caused by abnormalities in the ninth and twenty-second chromosomes. To win the CML lottery, one has to be fortunate enough to have both chromosomes break inside the same cell, and then a piece of one needs to fuse with the other, which forms a 9/22 hybrid chromosome known as the Philadelphia chromosome. That chromosome causes a rapid reproduction of the white blood cells containing the mutation and crowds out healthy white blood cells. Left untreated, the white blood cell production increases and eventually begins crowding out other blood cells. This ultimately leads to death or, in my case, an extreme inability to tolerate the mountains of Peru. Since red blood cells carry oxygen to the muscles and brain and my white cell count was elevated to the point where my red blood counts were low, my body was literally being starved for oxygen. I have read that certain people, like the Sherpas of the Himalayas and the Peruvians of the Andes, have evolved higher red blood cell counts to help them compensate for living at high elevations. I, on the other hand, had done the opposite—and then had climbed a mountain.

A few years before I learned of my CML, my dad and I had decided that we would try to go to a football game at each of the Big Ten football stadiums. That fall, while it was still unclear if the treatment would work, my dad and I went to several Big Ten football games in a mad dash to finish off the list. My dad went to law school at the University of Illinois. As an MSU Law grad, I was a Spartan by education, but I remained a Fighting Illini fan by birth. That year, Dad and I saw the Illini play at Michigan, Penn State, Indiana, and Wisconsin. The prior year, we had watched them lose the Rose Bowl after having watched them win at Ohio State. My relationship with my dad had been rocky for a long time; for a few years, in my late teens, I rarely spoke with him. The time we spent traveling to football games, both before and after my diagnosis, gave us a chance to work through our issues.

I survived until Christmas, but by then I wasn't ready to say goodbye. I was starting to think that I might be able to stick around a little longer; my doctors were optimistic about my prognosis, and the imatinib treatment was working as well as could be expected. I was taking 400 milligrams a day orally. A single large pill once a day was pushing back my death sentence. Unfortunately, imatinib is not a cure for CML—and I still wanted a cure. The only actual cure, according to my doctor, would be to get a bone marrow transplant—an extremely risky option where something like one in five people die within the first hundred or so days after the transplant. Still, I wanted to explore it. I didn't like the idea of having to take chemotherapy (imatinib is a targeted form of chemo) for the rest of my life. Because it was so new, the side effects of long-term imatinib use were unknown, and the short-term side effects of nausea, stomach pain, muscle cramps, and diarrhea were not exactly awesome.

That winter, I started looking into getting a second opinion. I had learned that it was very rare for people my age (I was only thirty years old) to have CML. I asked my oncologist who he would see if he had been diagnosed with CML at thirty, and without hesitation, he named a doctor at MD Anderson in Houston. I immediately told him that I would go see her. He cautioned me, saying that he wasn't even sure she took new patients and that it likely wouldn't be covered by my insurance, but I was not dissuaded.

In the spring of 2009, I hopped a plane to Houston, where I met with the doctor that my oncologist had recommended. In Houston, I had my second of three bone marrow biopsies. I also met with another doctor, whose specialty was bone marrow transplants. Both doctors confirmed that my treating oncologist's diagnosis and treatment plan were correct, and that I should stay the course. I went home disappointed. I had not fully understood when I left to go to MD Anderson that I was still hoping for a complete cure, but by the time I had completed my follow-ups with them, I understood that I had not yet fully accepted my lot. It would take another year and a second trip to see the Houston doctors before I'd finally accept that a transplant was too risky.

I still suffer from frequent diarrhea and am forced to face my mortality on a daily basis by taking a dose of imatinib. Fortunately, in the years since, my prospects have improved. I have tolerated the drug reasonably well, and my disease is at an undetectably low level. Plus, there are two newer targeted treatments I could try if my CML becomes resistant to imatinib.

After my first trip to Houston, I returned my focus to the law firm. Still down an attorney, I had been forced to cut back on new client intake to compensate. I was unable to adequately focus, and the increased costs associated with having to pay other attorneys to cover hearings had been piling up. Immediately after my diagnosis, I had been in a really bad spot professionally. I had a pile of cases with no active lawyer to cover them, and I wasn't able to attend court hearings for several weeks. I got through those crucial first few months with the help of my friend Travis.

I met Travis during my second year of law school. Travis had transferred to MSU Law after his first year at Cooley. I was a founder and the first president of the Conservative Law Society. CLS started when a few of us were talking about how there was a shortage of groups on campus that catered to conservatives. We proposed the new group to the school and were told it wasn't needed because it already existed. The administration believed that the Federalist Society was sufficient. Federalists believe in a conservative approach to interpreting the Constitution, and the school thought that one such group was enough. I refused to accept that and appealed the decision. I argued that while CLS generally agreed with the Federalists in Constitutional interpretation, we had some distinct differences. I pointed out that if there were to be a Constitutional amendment that clearly stated that women had a right to abortion, the Federalists, who thought *Roe v. Wade* was inappropriately decided, would by their own rules accept and support the amendment as proper Constitutional interpretation. We, on the other hand, would still oppose abortion and would work to revoke the amendment.

My arguments prevailed, and we were recognized in the spring of my second year at MSU. We had our first meeting and drafted a constitution of our own. Travis was at that meeting and had been instrumental in helping us form the group. I don't recall exactly when I first met him, but I know that by that spring we were fast becoming friends. That next year we would drink together, study together, and spend our free time playing Rich Dad's Cashflow 101, a board game that was created by Robert Kiyosaki to help people learn how to invest. Travis was actively investing and flipping houses in Metro Detroit and would head over that way a couple times a week to work on his business.

If not for Travis, I have no idea when, or if, I would have gotten actively involved in real estate. I had always been interested in it. I had read *Rich Dad Poor Dad*, and I had stayed up late watching real estate infomercials on TV as a teenager. However, in the decade or so since, I had yet to make any significant investments. I still owned the small house where Becky and I had gotten engaged, but I had rented that to a friend for below-market rent as a placeholder until I finished law school. I thought, at the time, that the most sensible plan was to wait to start investing until after finishing school and stabilizing our income. Then Travis came into my life, flipping his way through school and already owning several rentals. He was in his early twenties and already killing it in real estate. That spring, I committed a chunk of my student loan proceeds to a quick flip and made my first real estate investment as a fifty-fifty partner with Travis. That would be the first of many real estate investments Travis and I would make together, but it would also be the last one we would make for several years. Thanks entirely to Travis's efforts, I found myself suddenly flush with cash, and I did as I have often done: I promptly spent it. I'm not positive on the timing, but if my memory serves me correctly, it was just after we closed that deal that I took Becky to Europe for Valentine's Day on the trip where I would take her to see the *Moses*.

Travis would continue to invest and flip houses, even as the market crashed over the next several years, and by the time I was hospitalized with leukemia, he would be making big money by selling cash-flowing properties to buyers from all over the world. As near as I can tell, all through law school and all through the crash, Travis continued to make money flipping houses. It wouldn't be until my own personal crash that he would stop. When I got too sick to work and I didn't have an attorney to cover my cases, Travis stopped flipping houses. He spent his weekdays at our house, sleeping in our spare bedroom, and his weekends at home, managing his business as best as he could. Every Monday he would get up early and drive three hours to Grand Rapids to show up at my office. He covered hearings and met with my clients. He did damage control and kept me from losing my license to practice law. The judges and most of my clients were understanding, but my personal crash did nothing to slow their worlds. They needed representation, and Travis provided it. He refused to let me pay him. He just kept showing up and doing what he needed to do to make sure that I would make it through. I don't know how Becky and I would have handled those first few months without Travis.

February had come and gone, and my dad and I had not gone to Australia. Between doctor appointments and trips to Houston, I was beginning to get back to work. By the summer of 2009, I was starting to see a new problem on the horizon. The economy was crashing, and I had a serious shortage of clients. For several months when I first got sick, we had essentially stopped taking on new clients. That, combined with the Great Recession, was causing a perfect storm. We had sold our small house and moved into a bigger, more expensive house just before I got sick. We had used up all of our money and then some, just surviving the last ten months. Between January and August 2008, I had made nearly a hundred thousand dollars—that was more than ten thousand dollars per month. However, by the end of the year, my net income was negative—it was costing four to five thousand dollars each week to keep the doors open at the law firm, and we were not producing nearly enough money to cover it.

I needed a distraction, and for the first time in years, I didn't have enough money to plan a vacation. I started to bug my dad about his promised trip to Australia. He had stopped practicing law and had just moved his trucking company to Chattanooga, Tennessee, to be closer to an important client of theirs. The timing was off, and we wouldn't get a chance to go to Oz until February 2013, more than three years later. By then, I'd be living in Tennessee and working for Tom and Dad at their trucking company.

In the fall of 2012, when it became obvious to Becky and me that I would soon be going to Australia, the two of us decided to take scuba lessons. We both love to snorkel, and couldn't see going to the Great Barrier Reef and not diving. My dad had agreed to pay for my trip, including flights and hotels. I would be responsible for my meals. We planned to spend the entire month of February in Australia. Becky would get to fly over and join us for about twenty days in the middle of our trip. She would also get to dive the reef. Scuba lessons were everything I had dreamed they would be and more. The first weekend of class, we found ourselves eight feet or so down in the deep end of an indoor pool playing frisbee. Pool time is designed to get the diver familiar with the gear and the safety equipment in a low-risk environment, and I loved it. I loved sitting on the bottom of the pool, breathing underwater.

When we were kids, my brother and I would take deep breaths, grab on to heavy objects, and walk across the bottom of our pool. Sometimes we would stay under for more than a minute; one time I had even held my breath for a full two minutes. The first time I dropped over the edge of the deep end of the divemaster's pool, I stayed under for more than ten minutes, breathing comfortably. I could easily have stayed down for an hour. It was exhilarating, and I loved every minute of it. Not everyone who tries diving immediately loves it. It was harder for Becky than it was for me, and some people never learn to love it. For me, it was immediate love. After that first underwater breath, I would never go back. I still love snorkeling; in fact, as I write this, I am sitting in the lobby of the Caribe Hilton in San Juan, Puerto Rico, and I am about to pack up and go snorkeling in the protected cove on the property. Yesterday, Becky and I celebrated our sixteenth anniversary in the water, where we saw large schools of blue tangs, some reef squids, and a plethora of other tropical fish, including what appeared to be a giant pufferfish hiding in a hole in the rocks.

A little over sixteen years ago, as we prepared for our wedding, Becky and I decided that it would be fun for me to plan a surprise destination for our honeymoon. Becky had traveled much less extensively than I had, and she had never been out of the country except on one brief trip to Niagara Falls in Canada while en route to New York with a youth group. It was decided that she would apply for a passport, and I would plan our trip. I started researching potential trips that fell within our limited budget. After several days of searching the internet, I found cheap flights to San Juan. I had never been to Puerto Rico and was up for an adventure. I bought a guidebook and started planning a ten-day trip to the island.

At the time I was still working at 7-Eleven. I invited several of my regulars to our wedding, including Dawn, who sold cruises for a living. Almost as soon as I told her that I was getting married, she started talking to me about booking a cruise. I was very resistant. I didn't like the idea of being trapped on a boat with a bunch of tourists. I have never considered myself a tourist. I am a traveler. I try to immerse myself in the culture in which I travel, and cruising seemed, at the time, like the opposite of what I do. One day, Dawn came into the store and asked me if I had planned our honeymoon yet. I told her that I had bought tickets to San Juan, and she again mentioned cruising. I told her that I already had booked the flights and they were nonrefundable. She took it as a challenge to find a cruise for us that left and returned to San Juan during the ten days we would be there.

The next day, Dawn came to see me at work and told me that she had found a perfect option for us. The *Carnival Destiny* was embarking from San Juan on August 17, 2003, the very day we were scheduled to arrive. Over the course of seven days, we would visit St. Thomas, Martinique, Barbados, and Aruba. We would still get three full days to explore Puerto Rico. She had tried to convince me that a cruise was perfect for a honeymoon, and that my wife, who was less traveled than I was, wouldn't want to backpack around Puerto Rico for our honeymoon. While I am sure that she was right about that, I remained unconvinced—at least until she told me the price. The price she quoted for an ocean view room on the cruise was slightly cheaper than what I would have spent to stay in a hotel near Old San Juan for the same seven days. Plus, the cruise would include food and would take us to a number of new places. I booked the cruise.

Cruising is different from traveling, but different doesn't mean bad. We had a great time on the cruise. For our second anniversary, we returned to San Juan and took the *Carnival Destiny* a second time. Since that second cruise, we have done several more cruises. We have seen dozens of islands and have fallen in love with the Caribbean and with cruising. We have cruised the Nile River. My dad and I even cruised the South Pacific, visiting Vanuatu and New Caledonia in the Coral Sea. Cruising has allowed Becky and me to dive and snorkel in remote ports. We have met great people and have had incredible cultural experiences.

Most people treat a cruise like a floating buffet that drops them at a beach or a shopping mall. We do not. We eat well on the ship and sometimes do walk off the boat directly to a beach or mall, but we also try to explore. We rent cars and drive to remote parts of the island. One time in Mexico, we hired a driver to take us more than an hour into the jungle to a recently discovered Aztec ruin that was still being uncovered. Another time, we took a water taxi to Ambergris Caye in Belize and swam with sharks and stingrays. I still love to travel, but I also love the convenience and ease of a cruise. It has been nearly two years since the last time Becky and I have been on a cruise and more than a decade since we went on one leaving from San Juan, but that is about to change. Later today we will board a ship and head out. I am excited to return to some of our favorite ports, including St. Thomas and Barbados, but I am most excited to visit St. Lucia, a place we have not yet been to.

REFLECTION QUESTIONS

1. Do you think it would be harder to face potential death or potential financial failure?
2. Do you have someone in your life who would drop everything for you?
3. Who do you have in your life who's so important that you would drop everything for them?
4. Do you ever get set in your ways and automatically reject nonconforming suggestions?
5. Would you have booked the cruise?

Ten

THE BOTTOM

> I have never seen anything like this
> before locally, and it could be really bad.
> —Chattanooga News Channel 9 mete-
> orologist David Glenn, April 26, 2011

"**P**lease state your full name for the record." It was those words that marked the bottom for me. Just before I heard them, the bankruptcy trustee, a man whom I had appeared before hundreds of times in my professional capacity, had expressed his sympathy by saying that he was sorry to see me in front of him in this manner. I knew what would happen next and had done my best to prepare my wife for the hearing. But as I sat there, I just wanted to leave. I wanted it to all be over. I had never thought that I would be bankrupt in my early thirties. The two years following my diagnosis with CML had been a roller coaster. As we sat before the trustee, we were still current on our mortgage and on all of our credit card bills. However, the law firm's debts were drowning us, and we had racked up more than one hundred thousand dollars in unsecured debts, not including my student loans, which were non-dischargeable and totaled nearly another hundred thousand dollars. In spite of buying it right and spending thousands of dollars improving it, our house was barely worth what we owed. We were drowning in debt, and my income had still not recovered. I had failed.

When I was in high school, I had secretly declared to myself that I would quickly make $10 million. I planned to retire at the point where I had accumulated a net worth of $10 million adjusted for inflation into 1996 dollars (the year I graduated from high school). I had assumed that I would do this, at the latest, by the time I was forty. Following the bankruptcy, because of my non-dischargeable loans, at the age of thirty-two, I had a net worth around –$75,000—only $10,075,000 to go.

I had promised my wife that I would provide for her. If she helped me get through law school, I would give her the life of her dreams. Now, less than a decade after our wedding, I had caused her to go bankrupt. By the time we sat before the bankruptcy trustee, I had decided to close my law firm and had made the hard choice to take my wife away from her family and to move to Chattanooga. The hearing in which we sat was just one last step before we left town to start over. My dad had been repeatedly offering me a job in Tennessee for several years. Left with few other options, I made the hard choice to take it. When I finished my last shift at 7-Eleven, I had assumed that I would never have to work for someone else again. Now, just a few years later, I would be working for my dad. I had learned the hard way by working for my dad at his sawmill and working for my uncle at the sheet metal company: working for a family member is even worse than having a regular boss. And now, I would have to do it again.

In December 2010, a few days after our bankruptcy hearing, I signed a lease for a rental house in Chattanooga. I had no money and limited credit, but the landlord rented to several other people at my dad's company and took a chance on me. Keys in hand, I returned home to Michigan for the holidays and to wrap up the transfer of my law firm. I was scheduled to start my new job the first full week in January. Becky would stay at our house in Hudsonville until March and then would move down with the dogs to join me in Chattanooga. Her plan was to take a little time off while we settled into our new life in the South. I had committed to stay in Tennessee and work for my dad for a minimum of two years. In exchange for that commitment, he offered me a reasonable salary, a loan to buy a car, and periodic bonuses.

In March 2011, after three months on my own in Tennessee, Becky, Roxy, Chloe, and Stella joined me in Chattanooga. I was happy to have them home. The dogs loved the large, flat, fenced-in yard. Our Great Dane, Stella, took to running laps, while the two Chihuahuas enjoyed the Southern sun. On my thirty-third birthday, a month or so after the girls had moved down, I was scheduled to work at our office in Tunnel Hill,

Georgia. I was working a mid shift, which meant I was going in around 11 a.m. and working until around 8 or 9 p.m. We were under severe storm watches most of that day. In the evening after 5 p.m., the building would empty out and we would be left with just a small skeleton crew. That night, it was just me and Matt, Tom's son, who were still in the building. We were hearing reports about dangerous clusters of tornadoes, and Matt decided that we should close up and go home.

I was in the habit of stopping at a local Waffle House on my way home and picking up a to-go soda. When I had first moved to Chattanooga and Becky was still living in Michigan, I had eaten at the Waffle House almost every day. So often, in fact, that one of my coworkers had taken to calling me Waffles. One of the first times I went there, I ordered an omelet. The server asked me a question, but I wasn't able to understand him. His accent was too thick for me, and I asked him to repeat himself. Listening carefully, I was able to sort out that he had asked me if I "wanted pecan sauce with that." Unsure about what pecan sauce was and why I'd want it on an omelet, I responded in the affirmative. When he brought me a bottle of salsa, I realized that he had said "picante sauce."

There is a scene in *The 13th Warrior*, a movie based on Michael Crichton's book *Eaters of the Dead*, in which Antonio Banderas's character slowly learns the language of his captors. I thought of that scene often that spring as I slowly began to understand the locals. After a few months of repeated visits and of talking to Southern speakers all day at work, I was finally able to fully understand the servers and customers at the Tunnel Hill Waffle House. On the day of the storm, I stopped to chat briefly about the weather, took my Diet Coke, and hopped back on the road.

The sky was darkening and the rain suddenly stopped as I made the turn onto Cherokee Valley Road. True to its name, the road winds through a beautiful valley, and its rolling hills are populated by newer farm homes. There are steep ridges on both sides of the road. It was, and still is, a beautiful drive. It is a slightly less direct route home, but its remoteness and lack of traffic made it my preferred route. As I drove around a bend and was just about to enter the valley, a large tree blew down across the road and blocked my path. I pumped the brakes and was able to stop just short of the fallen tree. I heard a rumble and rolled down my window so I could hear it more clearly. The sound magnified significantly, and I watched in horror as trees began flying through the air in front of me. Then I saw what I can only describe as a gray wall of wind. My car began to rattle. I quickly turned around to head back toward Ringgold Road, an alternative route toward our rental house. That route was blocked as well, so I attempted to cut through downtown Ringgold.

Becky and I almost moved to Ringgold instead of Chattanooga. Ringgold is a small town about twenty-five minutes south of Chattanooga just off I-75 in North Georgia. We loved its old-timey feel. With a long and colorful history dating back to the Civil War, Ringgold is just a few miles from the site of the Chickamauga Battlefield, where one of the deadliest battles of the Civil War was fought. The town is also home to the historic Ringgold Depot, which is now an event center. Just off from the depot is an old railroad bridge. Heading north, I drove under the bridge in a futile attempt to get around the devastation all around me. There was no power, the lights were off, and the roads were empty, except for the odd person peeking out of a building or home.

I had called Becky before leaving the office and told her I was heading home, but it was now obvious that I wouldn't be making it home anytime soon. In the best-case scenario, I would have to drive an additional ten or so miles up I-75 and then come back down our road the same extra distance. It would be at least another thirty minutes before I could get home. I pulled over in the middle of the main thoroughfare, called Nashville Road. I used my cell to try to call Becky and got a busy signal. I tried several more times but wasn't able to get through. I tried to call my dad and my mom, hoping that one of them could get through to Becky, but again I got busy signals. Realizing that the cell towers were not properly functioning, I started driving down Nashville Road and was blocked by debris. I decided to cut back and head over to the Waffle House on the highway and attempt to take I-75 north. The interstate was also blocked. My phone rang; it was my dad. He said that there was a major tornado hitting Ringgold right now. I said I was in Ringgold. Before I could get him to call Becky, he said, "Okay, I better let you go then." After that call, it would be more than an hour before my phone would work again. I spent about forty-five minutes stopped on the highway talking to other drivers as we waited for them to clear the road.

Nervously looking toward the west, we talked about the damage we had seen. I learned that there had been a direct hit on the high school and that Cherokee Valley Road had been destroyed. The details slowly emerged, and it was obvious that we were only just beginning to learn how bad the storm really had been. Becky was at home just a few miles away, but I couldn't reach her. She was in the closet under the stairs, huddling with the dogs and listening to news playing on the television in the next room. As nervous as I was sitting exposed on the side of the interstate, Becky had it far worse. She had only just moved to the area, didn't have a job, and didn't have any friends, and all she had just heard was that a monstrous EF-4 tornado, over a half mile wide, had scored a direct hit on Ringgold. She knew I should have been home by now. She knew that I usually took Cherokee Valley Road, and she knew that the worst damage was there.

Twenty people lost their lives in or around Chattanooga that day, including several on Cherokee Valley Road. The local news would cover almost nothing else for weeks, but nationally the tornado was overshadowed by the even larger EF-5 tornado that hit Joplin, Missouri, just a few days prior at the start of what is now known as the 2011 super outbreak. The Joplin tornado marked the start of the outbreak, and the Ringgold tornado was one of the last. All told, there were 360 confirmed tornadoes and nearly as many fatalities.

I arrived home about two hours later. My commute, which normally took about twenty-five minutes, had taken more than three hours. I hugged Becky and told her of the destruction I saw and of the tornado that had shaken my car. As we hugged, we cried. We had been through so much, and Becky was already thinking of moving back home. We were lucky; our home wasn't damaged, and no one we knew was injured, but we were also scared. I had lived in Chattanooga for less than five months, and Becky had only been there a month. We had yet to make any friends, and now we were faced with unpredictable weather conditions. As we hugged, I thought about the future and about how to create a future of abundance. I was also happy. I was happy we were safe and that I had a job with good benefits that would cover my ongoing leukemia treatment. Mostly I was happy that I had my girls home with me in Chattanooga. I had not liked living alone. I missed my wife and my dogs and was comforted by their presence.

People say that bad things come in threes, but I was optimistic as we moved into the summer. The tornado outbreak had ended, my job was going reasonably well, and our bankruptcy was behind us. We were beginning to save up some money, and my profit-based bonuses from the trucking company were coming in higher than we had anticipated. It wasn't all good, though. That summer the last space shuttle launch was scheduled. I asked to take off from work, only to be told I couldn't go. I wasn't really getting along with my coworkers. I was missing the flexibility I had as an attorney. I was used to having a full-time assistant. I was used to being able to decide when I wanted to work—or if I wanted to work. Ever since I saw a space shuttle just after launch as a child, I wanted to see an actual launch. Now, I was missing the last one. As I write this, I still regret missing that launch. Having a job was saving my life and giving me a chance to get back on my feet, but it was also stealing from me. It was preventing me from living the life that I wanted to live.

The space shuttle consisted of a reusable orbiter strapped to several nonreusable rockets. From its first launch in 1981 and until July 21, 2011, when the last orbiter was retired, it remained the primary space vehicle for NASA astronauts. Since that time, the United States has not had a crew-capable space vehicle. Instead, we have relied on buying passage on the Russian-made Soyuz rocket. The Soyuz is a fully nonreusable rocket and recovery system. As of this writing, there are no reusable space vehicles launching astronauts into space. There are, however, several promising developments, and multiple private companies are competing to create crew-capable space vehicles. Currently, Elon Musk and SpaceX have been able to successfully launch US astronauts to the International Space Station utilizing reusable rocket boosters.

Dogs always seem to know when their people need them. I came home from work feeling bummed out about missing the last launch and was greeted by the three dogs. Roxy was particularly happy to see me. I spent a little extra time snuggling with her. She was the first dog I had as an adult, and we were completely bonded. Roxy Q and I settled in on the couch to watch some TV. As a puppy she would often climb up onto my shoulder and stick her nose into my neck. That night, perhaps sensing my sadness over what I saw as the demise of the US space program and over having missed that last launch, she acted like a puppy again. She climbed up next to my face and nuzzled into my neck. It would be the last time she would do so.

Just after midnight on the eighth anniversary of our wedding, Becky and I drove Q to the emergency vet. She had collapsed earlier in the day and had not been eating. Becky had taken her to the vet earlier and they had done some imaging, determining that she had a gas buildup. They gave Becky a gas pill, and Q wouldn't even take that. When I got home from work that day, I forced her to swallow the pill. She was unhappy with me, but since she trusted me, she swallowed the pill. A few hours later, she collapsed. We loaded her into the car and began her last drive. She lay on the seat between us and rested her head on my hand.

At the vet's office, we waited as they took her back for more testing. After what seemed like an eternity, they called us back and told us that her heart had stopped, but they had been able to stabilize her. They suggested that they monitor her for the remainder of night and that we come back later in the day to discuss our treatment options. We drove home in shock. She had seemed fine a few days before and was not yet eight years old. As I write this just over eight years later, she has been gone longer than she lived—and still the tears are streaming.

She was my dog, and I had to make the choice to end her life. I know that people say dogs go to Heaven and they are playing on the other side of the rainbow bridge, but I have never believed that. When I chose to end her life, I knew that I would never see her again. I didn't want to go back and watch it happen, but I had to do it. I had to say goodbye. I don't know what Roxy thought or felt as I said goodbye to her with tears streaming from my eyes. I don't know if she believed Becky when Becky told her it would all be okay, but I know I didn't believe it. I knew it would never be okay. I didn't want my dog to die. I still don't want her to be dead. I carried her tag on my keys for the next six years, and almost every day I teared up thinking about her. I love all three of the dogs we have, and as I write this I know in a lot of ways Trixie has stepped in to replace Q, but I don't think I will ever love another animal as much again. I miss her nearly every day. The third and final bad thing of that year had finally happened, and I would never be the same.

REFLECTION QUESTIONS

1. Have you ever had to completely upend your life?
2. Is it possible that drastic changes or life disruptions can be a benefit?
3. How would you deal with losing so much so fast (career, security, home, pet, etc.)?
4. How do you deal with loss? Can you do it and still find a way to live an extra ordinary life?
5. Can you grieve but still find a way to have an unbroken string of good days?

Eleven

FRESH START

You, me, or nobody is gonna hit as hard as life. But it ain't about how hard you hit. It's about how hard you can get hit and keep moving forward, how much you can take and keep moving forward.

—Sylvester Stallone, *Rocky Balboa*

The United States Bankruptcy Code is intended to give people a fresh start. At its best, when someone becomes so burdened with debt that there is no reasonable chance that they can get out of that debt, the Code steps in and gives them some relief. I had witnessed hundreds of people experience that relief in my days as a bankruptcy attorney, but I really didn't understand how it felt until I went through it. The pressure of my piling debt was suddenly gone, and I was able to start focusing on the future.

That fall, after Roxy's death, I wept frequently. Looking back, I can see that it wasn't all for my lost dog; it was also for my lost hopes and dreams. I was still focused on having good days, and I was still finding some positives every day, but it was harder than it had been in years. I was working a job, was taking daily doses of chemotherapy, had basically no assets, and still had a negative net worth. I missed my dog, but I also missed the life I had planned. I was no longer practicing law. I was living in a place where I didn't even have a license to practice. I was still searching for purpose. I felt many of the same things that I felt more than a decade earlier as I sat on the front steps of the church looking down on the Colosseum. I needed to find purpose.

Travis and I still talked regularly, and he was continuing to crush it in real estate. The market had crashed, and properties were trading for a fraction of what they had been worth a few years prior. Becky and I were saving money, and I wanted to put that money to work. I started talking to Travis about investing with him. I wanted to buy something. I wanted to build a portfolio that would ensure that no matter what happened to me, my wife would be fine.

By December 2011, we had saved up just over $20,000. Travis was keeping an eye out for a long term buy-and-hold deal that we could get in on. One day, he called me about a condo that we could buy for $30,000. It was a foreclosure and had previously been valued at over $100,000. It needed a few thousand in work before it could be rented, but he was to buy a duplex, and we were looking at a couple more deals. I was starting to realize that if I pushed forward with the real estate investments, I might be able to craft a life like the one I had longed for while watching Carleton Sheets infomercials as a youth. I figured if I kept working for a few more years for the company and kept buying real estate, I might create a business that would allow me some measure of financial freedom.

I had never really had a strong desire to go to Australia. It had always seemed interesting, and I wanted to see the kangaroos and koalas, but it didn't have the ancient sites that I preferred to visit. The trip ended up being so much more than I had expected. We landed in Sydney in the middle of the remnants of a tropical storm. It was basically a monsoon, and we spent the first day going to the movies. The next day, the weather cleared enough that we were able to go on a bit of a downtown walkabout. We took photos of the Opera House and Harbor Bridge. We took a ferry out to Manly Beach and back, and then headed over to Bondi Beach, taking a quick swim.

After a few days of touring Sydney, we boarded a cruise ship and took a ten-day tour of the South Pacific that would bring Dad and me to some of the most beautiful islands that I have ever seen. We snorkeled in New Caledonia and went scuba diving on a wreck in Vanuatu. On the day of the wreck dive, we were in Port Vila, the capital of Vanuatu. After getting back from diving, we still had a couple of hours before the ship was scheduled to leave. I wanted to try kava, a local tea-like drink said to have mild sedative and euphoriant properties. I have always loved reading travel memoirs, and it was in one called *Getting Stoned with Savages* by J. Maarten Troost that I had first heard of Vanuatu and of kava. My dad had zero desire to try it and just wanted to get back on the ship. So I hopped into a cab and asked the driver to take me somewhere I could try kava. He started to take me toward a local beach where they sold kava to tourists, and I objected. I wanted an authentic local experience and insisted he take me to wherever he went when he wanted kava. After some discussion and a short drive, we ended up in a dirt driveway.

I exited the cab and the driver pointed me toward a row of shrubs. I felt some apprehension; I was alone on the other side of the world, and no one other than a cab driver knew where I was. I looked around and didn't see any other people. I squinted my eyes in the sun and stared at the hedges before me. As I walked toward them, I thought about what I was proposing to do. Kava is a drug. It's not illegal in the United States per se, but it's also not exactly something that's well known in the US. I took pride in the fact that I had never smoked pot and wasn't a drinker before I was twenty-one years old. Yet here I was, half a world away by myself, preparing to drink kava. As I got closer, I was able to make out a break in the row of bushes before me, so I walked through. I came through into a small group of local men sitting in a half circle. The unexpected arrival of a sunburned white tourist caused a few of the men to stand, but several of them barely acknowledged me. Later, under the effects of kava, I'd realize that their failure to respond was probably a function of the fact that they were in a state of extreme chill.

The cabbie came through the bushes behind me and was greeted with near total indifference by the group of guys before me. He directed me to the left, where I saw a heavyset middle-aged black woman stirring a murky gray liquid in a large blue barrel with what appeared to be half of a boat oar. My driver said something to her, and she quickly dipped a half coconut shell into the sludge and handed it to me. I studied the liquid before me. It looked vaguely like dishwater. I sniffed it, and it smelled earthy. I wasn't sure exactly how one is supposed to take kava. By this point several more of the seated men had turned their attention toward me. One of them, seeing my hesitation, used his hands to pantomime, dumping the shell into his mouth. I took his meaning, hesitated for just long enough to mentally declare *When in Rome*, and gulped it down. It tasted worse than it looked and smelled, like a lukewarm tea brewed from a dirty bitter root and then stirred with a half canoe paddle in a used ninety-gallon trash can. There was no immediate change in my perception, and I hadn't really spent much time considering what to expect. My good friend Becca and I had read Troost's book as a kind of one-on-one book club and had talked about it on the phone a few times. When she learned I was heading to Vanuatu, she insisted that I should try kava. It was in her honor that I had dumped the nasty liquid down my throat.

The flavor was still lingering in my mouth. I asked a question I probably should have asked before consuming it: "What happens now?" The driver said that in about thirty minutes I would start to feel a warm sensation and that, a short while later, the world would slow down and that I would be hyperaware. He said that the best plan was to go sit in the circle and wait for it to hit me. I asked him if I should drink another to be sure that I had had enough. He laughed and agreed I probably should. Less than five minutes after my first shell, I gulped down a second. Immediately after, I told the driver I needed to go back to the ship. I wish I could have stayed and gotten to know the guys in the circle. I spent a few minutes shaking their hands and nodding at them before walking back through the bushes to the waiting cab. I still wasn't feeling anything from the kava, but it hadn't quite been thirty minutes when I got back to port. I started to feel the promised warmth as I was scanning my card to be let on the ship. I went back to my stateroom to wash off the residual salt from my dive. In the shower, the world slowed. I could suddenly feel every individual drop of water as it hit my skin. It was both a fantastic and a totally natural feeling. I wondered why I hadn't noticed the water in my previous showers. I dried off, savoring the feel of the towel on my skin, and then I lay down on my bed and slept. I woke up about two or three hours later and immediately felt regret. I should have stayed awake and enjoyed the experience, but instead I slept it off. It was the first and, thus far, the last time that I have had kava.

Becky flew to Sydney while Dad and I were still on the cruise and was there to greet us when we got back to Australia. From there, the three of us boarded a plane for Cairns, the gateway to the Great Barrier Reef. We booked a three-day, two-night stay on a liveaboard dive boat with ten dives, including two night dives. We had a few days before the boat was scheduled to leave, and we spent the time exploring the area to the north of Cairns. The dives were unlike any that we had experienced before. The Great Barrier Reef is the largest barrier reef system in the world. Becky, Dad, and I—along with my dad's wife, Joanne—had previously snorkeled with nurse sharks and stingrays on the second-largest barrier reef off the coast of Belize, but this was a whole new world. On one dive, we got turned around and ended up missing the main part of the reef. Becky and I knew we were off course but couldn't seem to get Dad to understand. It can be a challenge to communicate when you are underwater, and we were deeper than we should have been. Fortunately, all three of us had dive computers that automatically calculated our safety stops. After some wrangling, Becky and I were able to make Dad understand that we needed to slowly surface. Other than that dive, the trip was a great success. During one night dive, we saw a sea turtle that was about the size of a Volkswagen Beetle. We also saw jellyfish, sharks, and giant clams. There were coral walls and colors that were unbelievable. There were giant, playful fish that were as big as people.

On our second of two night dives, I was hovering about five feet above the sea floor and about forty feet below the boat, waiting as a few other divers ascended. It was dark. I could see the occasional beam of light from a fellow diver's flashlight, and I could see wherever I pointed with my own. I looked up and could see the lights on the bottom of the boat, which were there to make sure we could find our way back. I saw a shadow pass by. I lifted my light and pointed in the direction it went. I caught a glimpse of gray leather. I began slowly swiping my light back and forth. I saw the distinct dorsal fin of a shark, and then it was gone. I tapped Becky, who was also waiting to surface, and flashed my light on another large shark. The sharks appeared to be circling the boat about twenty feet above our heads. They were big—probably about seven or eight feet long—but they seemed much larger as they darted away from our lights. I checked my air. I had about 1,000 PSI remaining. My full tank had registered about 3,000 PSI. I had been down for about thirty minutes and probably could stay down another fifteen or so, as long as I controlled my breathing. I saw a flash of panic in Becky's eyes, and my breathing increased. There was no choice; we had to surface. There was no way we could wait out the sharks. I counted at least three, but I suspected there were more. I gave Becky a thumbs-up—diver lingo for "time to go up." She shook her head. I pointed to my air and gave her another thumbs-up. It was time to go.

The sharks continued to circle us as we slowly returned to the surface. I flashed my lights at them and noticed one shark barely a half dozen feet away. As I floated on the surface in the dark water, waiting as Becky climbed up the ladder into the boat, I thought about the sharks a dozen or so feet below and about the circumstances that had taken us to this point. Had I not gotten leukemia, and had I not been forced into bankruptcy, I would not be here in the warm water floating above the Great Barrier Reef. I wasn't scared. I was content. I was happy. I had a good life, and it was time to start moving forward. In a few days, Becky would head home to Chattanooga. Dad and I would rent a car and drive more than five thousand miles around the Australian continent. We would wake up early to spot platypuses in the predawn hours when they are most active. We would climb mountains and dodge kangaroos with the car. I can't say for sure that it was during those few moments floating in the dark sea that I decided to get back on track, but I know that by the time I returned home from Oz, I was ready to make bold moves. I was ready to build the life of my dreams.

REFLECTION QUESTIONS

1. What do you want from life?
2. What choice can you make now to move toward your goals?
3. What can you do today to point yourself toward your dream life?
4. What will it take to get you to move toward your own extra ordinary life?

to go with me to Florida to watch a rocket launch. He agreed, but he felt that if we were heading to Florida, we might as well take a few days of pool time at his condo as well. I didn't ask my dad for the time off. There was no one to tell me that I couldn't go. If my dad had said he didn't want to go, I'd have gone anyway. It had been almost a year since the last time I was in Florida. In March 2017, my dad and I had driven down to his condo and spent a few days relaxing in the sun before going on a cruise. Then I laid out by the pool rereading Robert Kiyosaki's excellent book *Rich Dad Poor Dad*. Occasionally, I'd check cryptocurrency prices on my phone or jump in the pool to cool off. It was the middle of the week, and I had nowhere to be. I was thirty-eight years old, and I didn't have a job. I wasn't looking for a job. A retired couple was in the pool that day, and I spent some time talking to them about their lives and about what had brought them to this point. I'm fairly sure that they didn't believe me when I told them that I didn't have a job and that I had no desire to get one.

I had ended my time at the trucking company the previous week and had no immediate plans to go back to work. Becky was still working, and we were able to get insurance benefits through her job. We had some savings but not enough to live indefinitely. I considered myself to be gainfully unemployed. I wasn't exactly retired, but I also didn't have to work. Becky and I had decided that rather than looking for a job, my time was better spent focusing on our real estate investments. Travis and I had parlayed our early investments and now had a significant number of units. To that point, we had rarely taken any money out and instead chose to reinvest the majority of our cash flow. My plan was to spend my time figuring out how to increase our cash flow by making new investments and by turning on the cash flow from our existing investments. With our savings and Becky's income, we weren't in immediate need of cash flow and probably could survive for a year or more. I figured I would spend that time doing some real estate deals and that those deals would make us enough that I wouldn't ever need to go back to a full-time job. I had craved the flexibility and freedom of not having a job, and now I was in a position to experience it. Dad and I were planning a cruise to celebrate. He had sold his company, and in doing so had become gainfully unemployed as well.

Becky was pragmatic about my desire to not work. On the one hand, I was essentially asking her to keep working while I spent my time going on cruises. On the other hand, she knew that I had always believed I could make more money by not working a regular job, and that I could get us closer to our goals if I were able to free up my time to pursue bigger and better real estate deals. In our first few years in Chattanooga, Becky had taken a break from working, and she felt I deserved a break as well. She also thought that there was a chance that I could figure out a way to make the kind of money we needed to support our lifestyle. Becky's income was enough that we were able to survive on it, but we didn't want to just survive— we wanted to thrive. I never planned to live an ordinary life, and I knew we wouldn't be satisfied living like everyone else. We wanted to travel. We wanted to live on a beach. We wanted to make sure that we never had to worry about money again. I knew that if we wanted to accomplish this, I would need to do more than get a job. I would need to do more than hang out at the pool. I need to create and execute a plan that ensured complete financial freedom.

Over the previous few years, while I was still working, I tried a number of different plans besides real estate to make my riches. I had it in my head that if we could make ten thousand dollars a month in passive income, we would be financially free. With that money coming in, we could live the rest of our lives however we wanted. I tried a multilevel marketing company. I started a computer business with Pete, and we were even awarded a patent for our technology—a software development tool that significantly reduces the time and costs associated with the creation of business applications. While working on these projects, I learned that if you want to be successful, you need to maintain focus. I also learned that I am not good at focusing on things that I am not passionate about.

This is a key point. It's much easier to focus on things you are passionate about. Long before I invested in real estate, I read books about real estate, I watched infomercials about real estate, and I thought about real estate. I love real estate. I love looking at deals and thinking about deals. I love the creativity involved, and I love the pride I feel when I drive by a building that I own. I never felt that about the computer company, and as a result, we were not successful. I still believe that our product has value and am hopeful that we can turn the company around. The problem is that I am merely hopeful; I am not passionate about it. I wish I were. I want badly to salvage it, but my time is better spent on my passions. When I focus on real estate, great things happen. If I focus on Newayva, the computer company, I get bogged down in the details and make little progress. Fortunately, the company is now marginally profitable, and we are no longer bleeding money. We have a few possible paths to recoup our losses, but none of them are certain, and my lack of passion about it means that I am not well enough informed to discern the correct way forward.

I learned a lot from Newayva and the other things I tried, but the most important lesson I learned was that I needed to focus on my passions. It was for that reason that I spent the first few days of my retirement sitting by a pool, rereading *Rich Dad Poor Dad*. That first year off of work, I read dozens of books and listened to many hours of real estate podcasts. Travis and I had been talking about investing in apartment buildings for more than a year, and I was determined to learn as much as I could about the economics of making the leap from single-family housing and duplexes to apartment buildings. There are tremendous economic advantages to investing in larger multifamily housing. The main advantage is the way they are priced. They are priced, like all commercial property, based on their net income. This means that if you buy poorly run properties, you can quickly increase the value by increasing the income they produce. This value-add strategy appealed to me as a way that I could push forward and produce the kind of income that Becky and I would need if we were to meet our goal of financial freedom.

Becky had taken nearly five years off when we had moved, and she was willing to let me do the same, provided that it didn't negatively impact our lifestyle. We both like to spend money. We go out for fancy meals and buy expensive consumer products. The money she makes is simply not enough to cover our current lifestyle. I figured that I needed to make about four to five thousand dollars a month in the short term in order to keep us from going backward. I set out to do that. My dad and I bought a run-down duplex in Chattanooga with a plan to fix it up, rent it, and refinance it. This method would allow us to build some serious equity and get most, or maybe all, of our purchase money back so that we could do another deal. We bought the duplex for around $50,000, invested another $25,000 in the rehab, and then we were able to refinance it. We got a loan for nearly all of the money that we had put in. We held that duplex for a few more years and then sold it for $185,000, making over $100,000 profit in just a couple of years.

I really wanted to start investing in apartments and was constantly on the lookout for them. Travis and I were looking in Michigan, and I was also looking in the Chattanooga market. I found a twelve-unit complex in Ringgold. It was on the side of town that had not been affected by the tornado. My dad and I were able to use the money we got from the duplex refinance to cover a large chunk of the down payment. Meanwhile, Travis and I located a nineteen-unit property in Eastpointe, Michigan, a suburb of Detroit. We closed the two deals barely a month apart, with me owning one-third of each deal. Just a little over six months after leaving my job at the trucking company, I was the proud owner of not just one but two apartment buildings.

Meanwhile, I was also struggling. I have struggled with my weight for my entire adult life. I had thought that once I stopped working, it would become easy for me to focus on exercise and healthy eating, but it was several months after leaving my job and I had not made any significant healthy lifestyle changes. I had to face reality. I was, and had been, making excuses. While working for the trucking company, my weight had ballooned to over four hundred pounds. As I had approached my early retirement, I had told myself over and over that once I finished working, I would have time to work out and to prepare healthy meals. I needed to turn it around. I love being alive, and it occurred to me as I was approaching forty years old, that I didn't know any four-hundred-pound fifty-year-olds. There could be no doubt: I was putting myself on track for an early death. I needed a better plan.

My good friend and commuting buddy Jason and I had made weight-loss bets as far back as law school. We still talk nearly every day. Often we talk about our lives and our goals. In one of our conversations that year as I prepared to leave my job, I told Jason that I figured I had about one year left to turn it around or I would have no choice but to undergo weight-loss surgery. Around that time, my primary care doctor brought up the possibility of weight-loss surgery. I told her that I recently retired and that I would be able to fix my issue on my own. She suggested that I join the weight-loss program at a local hospital. Even though I felt like I could do it on my own, I called the number she gave me and scheduled a consultation with a social worker who specialized in weight loss.

I don't often get nervous about meeting people, but I was apprehensive as I parked my car in the parking structure in advance of that first meeting. I exited my car and walked across the top level of a parking structure. It was very hot, and I wanted to take the elevator down the two flights to the ground level. Instead, I chose to take the stairs—not because I wanted the exercise, but because I thought that the social worker might be watching me arrive and waiting to see just how lazy I was. This was obviously not true, and even as I thought it, I knew there was no way that the weight loss center was posting people to watch the parking structure in hopes of catching an unsuspecting fat person taking an elevator. I entered the hospital through the front door and caught an elevator up the two flights to the weight loss and bariatric center. After a short wait, I was invited into a small office.

Since I was morbidly obese, I often struggled to find comfortable seating while in waiting rooms or doctors' offices. As I walked into the room, without thinking about it, my eyes scanned for a comfortable seat. It was small, and there was only one option—an extra-wide chair. The social worker, a slight man who appeared to be about sixty years old, welcomed me. He asked me to be seated and introduced himself. He started by asking me about my eating habits and past diets. I proudly told him about all the various methods I had tried and the many times I had lost thirty or more pounds on a diet, but I was forced to acknowledge that what I was doing was not working. Every time I lost weight, I gained back at least as much. As a result, my weight had been steadily rising for the last two decades. I looked at him and felt at peace. There was no judgment in his eyes.

As far as my obesity is concerned, I have been fortunate. Even at my highest weight of 420 pounds, I never had significant mobility issues. I didn't have high blood pressure or diabetes, but I also knew that the odds were not in my favor. I was blessed with good genetics and a large, strong frame, but I was also tempting fate. In that first meeting, he asked me about weight-loss surgery, and I told him that I didn't want to talk about it. I told him that I was not going to fail. He shared with me the depressing statistic that only about 5 percent of people who are morbidly obese are able to lose the weight and keep it off. I responded that I would be in the 5 percent. As I said those words, I thought about my decades-old choice to be happy and not to have bad days. I figured that I could easily do it again. I just needed to believe it.

Given his line of work, I am sure that I am not the first person to make such a bold statement, but he did not object. He did not argue with me. Instead he made some positive suggestions and gave me some pointers. He set me up to meet with a nutritionist and scheduled a follow-up with him for a month later. Depressingly, the nutritionist was impressed with my understanding of nutrition, which meant that I wasn't going to learn my way out of obesity. I knew how to eat healthy, but I simply was not doing it. I had never loved to exercise, but I was once fairly fit. I had spent three years swimming varsity in high school, and I knew how to exercise. Some people eat poorly because they don't know any better, but that was not my problem. I knew what to eat, I knew how to exercise, but I still wasn't making any progress.

I continued to see the social worker monthly for more than a year. Each time I spoke with him, I felt like I was making progress. I tried to understand what he was saying and to appreciate that he had experience and training that I had not been exposed to. Sometimes, I find it hard to learn from people I perceive to be less successful than me. I have always enjoyed reading books by ultra-successful people, and I love talking to people who have had great financial successes, but it can be hard for me to learn from people who are not famous or rich. Still, I chose to listen to this man. I chose to accept that he had knowledge beyond what I had. It wasn't easy. He came from a different background than me and had different political views than I did, but I still listened to him. I read books that he recommended, and I tried to grow. I realized that what I was doing wasn't working, and it was possible that this humble man had knowledge and experience that I did not have.

In the first month, I had talked over the nutritionist and had bragged about my knowledge of diets, but this man was telling me that it wasn't about diet. It wasn't about knowledge. It wasn't even about action. It was about acceptance. It was about managing a disease. I was obese. I suffered from the disease of obesity, and I always would. He told me about studies that proved that losing weight permanently slows down the formerly fat person's metabolism. It turns out that a two-hundred-pound man naturally burns about two thousand calories a day, but a formerly three-hundred-pound man who loses one hundred pounds burns far fewer calories a day at his new two-hundred-pound weight and therefore is much more likely to gain weight. In fact, if they both eat two thousand calories a day, the formerly fat person will quickly gain weight, while the first man will just maintain his existing weight. He told me about brain scan studies that showed obese people have significantly different reward-processing reactions. Obese people's brains react differently than those of thin people when they are showed images of sweet and fatty foods.

Looking back now, I sometimes wonder how he put up with my arrogance. I was so sure that I could do it the "natural way." I had convinced myself that surgery was a form of failure. To his credit, he never mentioned surgery as an option after that first day when I told him I was not interested in pursuing it. Over the next year, he talked to me about my life and my goals. We didn't just talk about weight loss and exercise; we talked about my entire life. I told him about how I wanted to be an apartment complex owner. I told him about my travel plans and my relationships with friends and family. The best part about the time I spent talking with him is that he never judged me. He believed in me. When I told him I wanted to buy apartment buildings, his response was that he "had no doubt that I would own apartments." It's rare in life to have someone support you unconditionally. I have been blessed with many great relationships, but having an outside person to talk to about your life can be very empowering. I had avoided these types of relationships. Even when I got sick, I had passed on the cancer support groups; I didn't feel like they would benefit me. But these monthly meetings did benefit me. I learned a lot about myself. After a while, I came to a conclusion: the only way I could fail was if I refused to make the right course corrections.

When a rocket is launched, there typically are a couple of initial engine burns. These burns put the rocket on the general course toward its goal, but once it hits orbit, the computer calculates its trajectory and nearly always initiates additional burns to correct its course. Sometimes these secondary burns are minor, but other times they are major course corrections. I was in need of a major course correction. After more than a year of monthly meetings, I had gained about one pound. I hadn't lost any weight and had gained a pound. This was something of a win. In the previous years, I had gained far more. I had made a course correction. I was a little less off course, but a small burn wasn't going to do it.

I thought about an attorney I knew back in Grand Rapids before I got sick and before I moved. He had chosen the gastric bypass. He was nearly sixty years old when he told me that after dieting for a full year, he was only down one pound. I thought about a coworker at the trucking company. She had gastric sleeve surgery and had lost more than one hundred pounds. I thought about a customer at 7-Eleven who had surgery and lost half his weight. I thought about a couple of relatives of mine who had undergone weight-loss surgery. Some of these people had lost incredible amounts of weight. Some gained it back, but others had not. I had told Jason that I had one year to lose the weight naturally. When I said those words, I felt that surgery would be a failure, but I see it differently now. Surgery is a tool. Surgery is a treatment option. Even though we never again talked about surgery, my monthly meetings had pushed me to grow as a person. I was beginning to accept that I couldn't do everything on my own. It's popular in the self-help and guru circuit to talk about self-reliance. Many of the gurus imply that you can will yourself to a better you. I had started the year feeling that I was capable of doing anything I set my mind on. I felt that I could choose to be healthy in the same way that I could choose to be happy and choose to give up on bad days. I thought that I could just make a choice and I'd magically stop binging on cheeseburgers and would fall in love with the gym. I tried very hard to make that choice, and more than a year later, I hadn't lost any weight.

On the positive side, I was working out more. I was walking and stretching regularly, and I had stopped gaining weight. I had also made the transition to apartments, and we were moving forward on our third complex, but I hadn't solved my obesity. I had to face the fact that I could not do it on my own. When I brought up surgery at my next monthly session, I felt a great relief. I didn't feel like a failure. It felt like I was forming a plan. I was setting something in motion. It was no different than when I started planning to buy apartment buildings. I had made a choice to lose weight and get healthy, and the best possible strategy for me was to explore my surgical options. It would take six months before my insurance company would approve my surgery, but the day that I chose to move forward changed my prospects. It was that day that I ignited the rocket and set my course toward a healthier me.

REFLECTION QUESTIONS

1. What are some areas in your life where you need to think about changing your position?
2. Are your thoughts and beliefs holding you back?
3. Are you willing to consider a major course correction?

4. Do you feel like you are excelling in one area but failing in another?
5. What or who can you turn to for help in achieving your goals?

Thirteen
YOU CAN DO IT

If you opt for a safe life, you will never
know what it's like to win.
—Richard Branson, *Screw It, Let's Do It*

I regularly drive from Chattanooga to Grand Rapids. A significant portion of my family and friends still live in my original hometown. When I was still working, I made the trip three or four times a year and would stay for four to five days before immediately heading back home to Chattanooga. Now that I don't have a regular job, I do the trip five or six times a year and spend a week or more each time. People often ask me why I don't just fly, since the ten-to-twelve-hour drive each way significantly reduces my time in the area. In response, I usually tell them about the time I flew to Grand

Rapids via Chicago and missed a connection. That time it took nearly ten hours to get there, but there are other reasons that I prefer to drive. I like the flexibility associated with driving. But the main reason was that when I was 420 pounds, getting on a plane even for a short flight was just not comfortable. Plus, while driving, I get more time to listen to audiobooks and podcasts. The first summer of my voluntary unemployment, I made more than one trip up. On one of those drives, I listened to Richard Branson's book *Screw it, Let's Do it*.

I first became aware of Richard Branson around the time I was in law school. It was then that he started selling tickets to space. It was the dawn of space tourism. This was before the end of the shuttle program, but it had been more than forty years since the last moon landing. I had been super excited a few years prior to that when Dennis Tito paid $20 million to become the first space tourist. But I was even more excited when the brash British billionaire announced that he would soon be launching people to suborbital space for a mere $250,000. Unfortunately, as of this writing, space tourism still remains decidedly rare, but with SpaceX, Virgin, Blue Horizon, and others being funded by a club of billionaires, it seems increasingly likely that this will soon change.

That fall, when Travis and I were discussing whether to move forward with the purchase of our nineteen-unit property, Branson's words pushed me forward. At one point as we were trying to decide if we should buy it or walk away, I said, "Screw it, let's do it." Around that time, I saw a meme that purported Branson had said that the difference between successful people and everyone else was that successful people took action before they had all the necessary information. I don't know if Branson actually said those words, but I do know that his book and that meme pushed me forward as I moved into the fall.

One thing that I know for certain is that success can only be achieved by action, and it is inaction that leads to regret. It's impossible to succeed at anything if you do not take action, and my biggest regrets have been over the things I did not do. I gazed across the waters at Morocco but did not hop the ferry across the strait. I spent years dreaming about real estate investing, but it wasn't until I had a cancer diagnosis and a bankruptcy behind me that I started buying rental properties. There is no way to know with certainty what would have changed for me if I had started investing sooner. However, I do know that had I invested when I first considered it, I'd have more than a decade of additional experience. It's even possible that the investments I could have made would have prevented me from going bankrupt. But what could have been doesn't matter. The key is to learn from your regrets, to learn from your experiences. A quick look back is healthy and can push you forward, but it's important not to spend too much time reflecting on the past. If you spend too much time looking back, you run the risk of not moving forward. It's essential to live in the present and to be looking toward the future.

You need to prepare for your future. You need to construct your dream life. No one else is looking out for you. The government and Social Security are not going to bail you out. Your job and its pension are very unlikely to be enough. When I was in Beijing, right before the COVID-19 pandemic began, I met an American couple who work as prison guards for a Midwestern state. They are both in their mid-forties and are expecting full pensions in their early fifties. I hope for them that it works out, and it might—but it also might not. Their state may simply not have the money to pay them, or, more likely, their fixed-benefit pensions will not keep up with inflation. The federal government has so much debt that inflation is inevitable at some point soon. Already we have seen a dramatic erosion of purchasing power. If your income and investments fail to keep pace with inflation, you become less wealthy. There are many more millionaires today than there were in the 1980s, but what does the title mean? Is a million dollars enough? What does it take to live your dream life? For me, a million is not nearly enough, and I doubt that it is for you either. If you had a million dollars today, you could probably safely take an income stream of $40,000 or maybe even $50,000 per year without reducing the principal. Let's say you are comfortable living on $50,000 per year before taxes. Let's say that you plan to live another twenty-five years or more. What will that $50,000 be able to buy in twenty-five or thirty years? Will you be comfortable living on that amount then?

Here's something to consider: if you had $50,000 to spend in 1990, you would have needed over $90,000 to buy the same amount of goods and services in 2017. This is the result of inflation averaging just over 2 percent a year. What if inflation goes back up? I originally wrote these words in 2019, but by early 2022, inflation has skyrocketed and was just clocked at more than 7 percent. The Federal Reserve continues to state publicly that this is a COVID-related transitory situation, but term value, not a paycheck. The worst deal that most people make is that they trade five-for-two over and over. Working five days so that you can have two days off is a bad trade. You need to craft a plan that will let you take months or years off of work. The only way to do that is to create residual, inflation-protected value. One strategy is to invest in cash-flowing real estate. Real estate prices rise with inflation. Yes, they can (and do) go down for periods of time, but it costs much more to buy a house now than it did in 1990 or 1950. Rents also go up with inflation. How much did it cost to rent an apartment in 1980? How much does it cost now? This book isn't intended to convince you to invest in real estate. The point is to make sure that you are taking whatever steps necessary to craft your ideal life. There are plenty of other possible assets available to you, but it's important to think about what your goals are and what really qualifies as an asset. Real estate isn't always an asset. It can also be a liability. Businesses aren't always an asset; they can also be liabilities. The key is to buy or create assets that produce predictable long-term inflation-adjusted returns. If you buy a house that rents for less than it costs you to keep it, then it takes money and time from you. That is not an asset. An asset gives you money and frees up your time. If you are an attorney and only make money when you work, then your law firm is not an asset. It's a liability. It takes your time—and if you don't give it that time, it forces you into bankruptcy.

My law firm was a giant liability. At the time, I thought that it was an asset because I was making good money, but it was a job with a liability attached. This doesn't mean that all law firms are liabilities though. If a person owns a multi-attorney law firm that pays them even when they don't show up to work, then that business is an asset. The fundamental principle is the same across all possible assets. This book could be an asset. I have spent some of my time writing it, and once I am done, I will put it out into the world. It could be an asset that produces money for me, but it might not be. If I don't sell many copies, I won't get any money back from it. If I print a bunch of copies and they don't sell, I could lose money or I could be forced to personally go sell them, which would take my time. In those scenarios, this book could be a liability. It could take my mental and physical energy and not produce a return. There are a number of ways this book could be a good asset for me. It could serve as a marketing tool to help me grow my real estate and real estate coaching businesses. It could help me find more investors or better deals. It could sell millions of copies and generate an inflation-protected stream of revenue for a long period of time. But the good news for me is that I don't actually care. I didn't write this book to be an asset; I wrote it because I want to help *you*.

If this book never sells and ends up being a liability, it's not a big deal to me, because I already have assets that produce cash flow. The biggest reason that you need to immediately start accumulating assets is that once you have enough assets, and once your predictable income from those assets exceeds the cost of your lifestyle, you can afford to accumulate liabilities as well.

The house I live in is a liability. It costs me money every month to live there, but it's okay because I have the money to pay for it. I can choose to spend my cash flow on liabilities. If you want to drive an expensive car and you can afford it, then you should drive an expensive car. But keep in mind that if you need to work a job to afford that car, then you can't actually afford it. You need to go buy an asset that produces the necessary cash flow to pay for the car. True financial freedom only comes when your assets produce more income than your liabilities consume.

I could probably write an entire book about real estate and how I went from bankrupt with no credit to retiring in less than a decade, but the nuts and bolts of that are beyond the scope of this book. The point is that I did it—and if I can do it, so can you. We had to get creative after those first few deals because we didn't have any more money to invest. We had to come up with novel structures, and I had to trust Travis and his team, but in the end we had to just keep moving forward. We made a choice to take action. We made that choice before we had all the possible information. We made the best decisions we could with the information that we had and moved forward.

Earlier this week, I met with an aspiring real estate investor. I told him a little about my story, and he was impressed with what I have done and what I have accomplished. He seemed jealous of my life and my experiences. I talked with him about my coaching program and the ways that I could help him move forward with his investment goals. I don't know if he will hire me or not. I know I can help him, but a significant part of me wishes that I could trade places with him. He is twenty-five years old, does not have leukemia, and has a good income. Knowing what I know now, I'd love to be twenty-five again and making more than $50,000 a year. I'd love to start investing now at an earlier age. I'd likely be able to travel more and to invest more. I'd definitely waste less time. But here's the thing I do know—I have a pretty great life at forty-three, and while I would like to be twenty-five again, I also am super optimistic about the future. I have goals and aspirations. I am currently pursuing additional apartment units. I am putting together and working on bigger and bigger real estate deals. My coaching business is taking off. I have the free time and energy to share my story. I do speaking engagements and am writing this book. I have formed great relationships with new investors all around the country. I have tapped into an engaged investment community in my adopted hometown of Chattanooga. I am in the process of potentially relocating to Puerto Rico. I have partnered with another friend to start the *Old Fashioned Real Estate™ Show*, where Brian Levredge and I drink bourbon old fashioneds and talk about real estate investing on YouTube (please take a minute and subscribe to our show www.youtube.com/oldfashionedrealestate).

I lost just under one hundred pounds and am working on a plan to make the remaining course corrections necessary to push myself even lower. In 2019, I went to China. A week before that, I was in Puerto Rico having a chat with the famed economist Harry Dent Jr. The week before that, I shook hands with Robert Kiyosaki, the author of *Rich Dad Poor Dad*. I even told him about my then upcoming trip to Tanzania, where my brother, a couple of friends, and I planned to climb Mt. Kilimanjaro (see the epilogue). In 2020, like all of us, I traveled much less overall, but when I visited Africa in February and Yellowstone in June, I got to see what it was like without the crowds. In 2021, I spent more than two months in Puerto Rico and now have a place there.

The reason that I get to live this life is that I made a choice to move forward toward my dream life. When I held the knife against my wrist, I realized that I didn't want to die. I realized that I wanted to live. When I first glimpsed Michelangelo's *Moses*, I realized that I wanted to live an extra ordinary life, but it wasn't until I got sick and faced death that I realized that I had to do it now. If I had taken the usual course, my life would be following the usual path. Instead, I am living my dream life, and there is nothing I want more than to help other people live their dream lives. It is the reason that I do what I do. I have finally found my purpose.

I could sit back and cash my rent checks. I could go live on a beach and dive every day with my wife, but instead I spend my time writing and speaking, telling people my story in the hope that it will help and inspire them. I spend time creating investment opportunities in the hope that my investors can use their returns to craft their dream lives. I coach a small group of real estate investors and businesspeople on how they can build their businesses in a way that allows them to live an extra ordinary life. I also created a new show, *Last Life Ever*, where we interview people living their best version of themselves; please subscribe wherever you listen to podcasts. For more information about *Last Life Ever*, see appendix A.

Everything I do now is designed to inspire myself and the people around me to live their dream lives. It's your last life until the Resurrection, and you need to live it now. Carpe diem—Seize the day! Live your best life now! You will eventually face your death. It's going to happen. At some point you will draw your last breath. I hope and pray that it will be many, many years from now. At the end of the day, when you are lying on your deathbed, you will not regret the things you did. But you absolutely will regret the things you did not do. Only you can know what it is that makes up your dream life, but whatever it is, you have to do it now. Make sure to live your life like it's your last life ever. I know you can do it. If I can live this extra ordinary life, you can too. Don't wait until you get leukemia or go bankrupt, and don't dwell on the past. Take action now. Don't wait until you have all the possible information. It's your last life ever, and you have to live it now.

Epilogue

TEN MORE FEET

I wrote the following essay for a *Last Life Ever* book called *Coronavirus Collective*, which is a collection of inspiring essays written from the center of the COVID-19 storm. It is an amazing window into the inner workings of some truly extra ordinary people, and I am so happy that I got a chance to share my thoughts as part of that collection. If you have not read it, I highly recommend checking it out.

Just after waking on the second day of February 2020, I went to my kitchen and swallowed an anti-malaria pill. Unlike most of the rest of the world (outside of China), I knew that my life was about to change. I had gone over my emergency supplies—antibacterial hand wipes, emergency food, more than a month's supply of medication, and thousands of dollars in cash. I had it all on hand and packed. I was ready to walk out my front door, and I knew I wouldn't be back until March. That same day, the first COVID-19 death outside of China was reported: a forty-four-year-old Wuhan resident died in the Philippines. I had been planning for this day for more than a year and had been thinking about it for a decade.

Later that day, wearing a backpack and carrying a large duffel, I was dropped off at the airport and checked in for my flight. I had packed and repacked my bags more than half a dozen times over the last few weeks. On my feet, I wore barely broken-in hiking boots that I bought to replace the ones that I had determined were a touch too small. The first leg of my journey was a short hop to Atlanta. We landed on time, but there was a delay getting to the gate, and I barely made my connection to Amsterdam. I worried about my checked bag, which contained the majority of my gear, including most of my emergency supplies. Another short connection and I was on a plane to Nairobi. My plan was to stay there a single day and then head to Ethiopia.

After landing in Nairobi, I descended the stairs onto the African tarmac. The late evening air was dry and hot. When I left my house only twenty-four hours prior, it had been a cold, crisp winter afternoon. When I landed it was summer in the Southern Hemisphere. Nairobi is about 125 miles south of the equator and sits at just under six thousand feet in elevation. I took a deep breath and tried to determine if I could feel any difference in the air. It seemed the same. In Amsterdam, as I had wandered through the crowded airport searching for my gate, I don't recall seeing a single person wearing a mask. But as I climbed up the stairs and toward the terminal building in Kenya, I saw guards wearing masks and checking passenger temperatures. I stood still as the Kenyan guard checked me for fever and worried about my bag and about my passport. I had been to China just a few months prior, and I was afraid that seeing the Chinese visa in my passport might subject me to increased scrutiny at a time when I just wanted to get my bag and go to my hotel. I wanted to rest. It was already ten at night, and I still needed to find my bag. I cleared customs quickly— they barely glanced at my passport—and I was waved to the baggage claim only to learn that my bag was somewhere over the Atlantic en route to Amsterdam.

With barely thirty-six hours until my flight to Ethiopia, it was essential that I got my bag as soon as possible. I needed my food, gear, toilet paper, and hand wipes. I distracted myself the next day by doing a quick tour of Nairobi. It was my first time in Africa outside of Egypt. I had hoped to see some wildlife, but instead I saw a run-down museum, a sprawling city, and an impoverished slum. I returned to the airport the next morning, February 5, and was relieved to find that my bag had arrived—just in time for me to recheck it to Addis Ababa, the capital of Ethiopia. Upon arriving in Addis Ababa, I repeated the ritual I started in Nairobi: I paused briefly to take in a deep breath of slightly cooler, winter air. I had spent less than two days in the southern summer. This time the air felt different. I struggled ever so slightly to catch my breath as I climbed back up to the terminal building. I'd spend the next four days acclimatizing to the new, higher elevation. It was all part of my plan. I had a mountain to climb and needed to make sure I did it.

On February 9, the day the death toll in China rose to 811, officially surpassing the number of fatalities recorded in the 2003 SARS outbreak, my brother and my high school friend Rick landed in Addis Ababa for a short layover on their trip to Tanzania. I joined them at the airport. We drank delicious local coffee and talked about how our world was about to change. The three of us boarded a plane and flew to Tanzania. Six days later, on Valentine's Day, around 4:30 in morning, I heard my brother climb back into our tent. We were camped at just over twelve thousand feet, three days into an eight-day climb to the top of Africa. I climbed out of my sleeping bag and out of the tent. I stood quietly in the dark, cold air and looked up at the peak of Kilimanjaro still more than seven thousand feet above me. I was worried. I had been struggling to keep up with the group. I drew in a breath and thought about the thinness of the air. I thought about the way it felt in my lungs. I looked down into the valley at the lights coming from Moshi, but mostly I looked up at the mountain above me. I was on a quest. For years I had wanted to summit this particular mountain. I am not a mountain climber, and at twelve thousand feet I was already approaching the highest elevation I had ever experienced. I was worried I would get mountain sickness and be forced to return without ever reaching the peak, but I was even more worried I would simply give up. The climb was much harder than I anticipated. I had known that the last push to the summit would be difficult, but I hadn't fully understood how hard the first few days would be. By the second day of the climb, I had already begun to consider the possibility that I wouldn't make it. As I stood alone in the quiet camp, watching the day slowly approach, I had a choice to make. Later that same day, Egypt would report a single case of COVID-19—like me, the virus had made it to Africa. Today, as I write this, I have a choice to make. I can choose to continue, or I can choose to give up. I can choose to use this time to better myself and to keep moving forward, or I can stop and wait for it all to be over. No one would have blamed me if I had stopped my climb. My life would not have been ruined. I would still be me, but I also would have known I could have done more. I would know that I quit. I would know that I failed. So, I chose to keep moving forward. I chose to push myself. I chose to keep making progress toward my long-held goal of standing at the highest point in Africa. It was by no means certain that I could make it to the top. It was overwhelming to realize that so much of my potential success was completely out of my control. It's not possible to know how many people successfully summit Kilimanjaro. Most tour companies claim success rates in the 80 to 90 percent range, but it is commonly believed that the true success rate is around 65 percent. A significant number of those who attempt to climb the mountain but do not summit succumb to acute mountain sickness, a potentially fatal disease that can cause swelling on the brain or fluid-filled lungs. The risk of getting sick can be minimized, but not eliminated, by taking your time, walking slowly, and following the maxim to climb high and sleep low. The body needs time to adjust to elevation or it dies. Some people naturally adjust to elevation more quickly than others, but we all need time to adjust.

That morning I chose to keep walking. Throughout the rest of the climb, I kept choosing to move forward. As people passed me on the mountain, and as my group waited for me to make it to camp, I continued to choose to keep walking forward. It was a thousand small choices that got me through that day and to the next camp. My mind kept telling me that I could stop. I could tell the guides that I had a bad headache that wouldn't go away, a classic sign of a high altitude cerebral edema. With symptoms like that I would be forced to descend quickly. More importantly, I would save face. Getting sick and being forced to lower altitudes would not be considered a failure, but instead a prudent response to a life-threatening illness. I wanted to quit, and I knew that I could fake the symptoms necessary to save while doing it, but I also wanted to make it to the top. I wanted to prove to myself that I could do it. I had a choice to make, and I chose to keep walking.

On February 16, around 6:00 p.m., I was awakened when our guide opened our tent to check on my brother. He had been wheezing and coughing since the previous night, and they were monitoring his blood oxygen levels. After lunch that day when we went to our tents to rest (we would begin the final push to the summit that evening with the hope of being on the crater rim of the great volcano in time for sunrise), my blood oxygen level was in the mid 80s—low, but not outside of the normal range for someone camped above sixteen thousand feet. My brother's blood oxygen levels had been in the low 70s. However, when they woke him, it was in the mid 50s—a dangerously low level that meant he needed to descend immediately. He would not be summiting, but he also did not fail. He had pushed himself beyond his body's limit. Later, while recuperating in the hospital, he would be told in no uncertain terms that if he had attempted to continue, he would have died. While he was getting ready to leave and head down, I asked him if he wanted me to descend with him, and he told me to go back to sleep.

I was worried about my brother. I was worried that I would give up. I was not able to sleep, and at nine that evening, having gotten only a couple hours of sleep, exhausted and already struggling to catch my breath, I pulled on my layers. I hadn't showered in seven days. My fleeces stank, but I barely noticed them as I layered one on top of another. I slipped into my snow pants, and put on my down jacket and my raincoat. I climbed out of my tent and stumbled over to the mess tent for a cup of coffee. The plan was for me, a single guide, and a summit porter to leave two hours ahead of the rest of the group in the hope that we would end up reaching the crater rim at approximately sunrise.

Precisely at ten, I left camp with my guide, Ponse, and my personal summit porter, Baltius, and began to climb. It took me until 8:11 a.m. to reach the summit. En route I had been passed by dozens of climbers who had started after me, and the rest of my group caught up with me and passed me at around 5 a.m. I so badly wanted to quit. My feet were aching (I ended up losing both of my big toenails), and my legs felt as if they could no longer move. I was both freezing cold and sweating. As we zigged and zagged up the dark mountain, my headlamp illuminating the path, I would look only to the next corner and think to myself, *You can do this. It's only ten more feet.* I stumbled and staggered. Finally, after what seemed like hours, I would reach that next corner. I'd lean on my trekking poles, close my eyes, and take a micro-nap. On one of these short rest breaks, I fell completely asleep while still standing up. Baltius, who spoke almost no English, came up behind me and softly played his harmonica. I woke up to the music, looked ahead at the next corner, unable to see what lay beyond, and thought, *I only need to make it ten more feet.*

We live in an uncertain time. We don't know what will happen next. We all have a choice to make. Will we keep moving forward? We each have to make that choice, but we are not in this alone. I would not have made it to the top of Kilimanjaro if not for Baltius and his harmonica. We need to find people to support us as we move forward. We cannot see what is coming. We can only see the path that's lit before us. We can only see the next little bit, but if we keep moving forward at our own pace, with the support of loved ones and our friends, we will get through this. We are all facing an illness over which we have little or no control, but we can take steps to minimize its impact, and we can keep moving forward. We only have to make it ten more feet.

Appendix A

LAST LIFE EVER

When I wrote most of this book in the summer and early fall of 2019, I was still trying to figure out what I wanted to do with my life. I knew that I wanted to figure out a way to help even more people. It's the reason that I started taking investors into my deals, it's the reason that I started telling my story, and it's the reason I started writing this book—but I wasn't sure how I was going to do it. As I mentioned in the last chapter, I was planning to release a show called *Last Life Ever*. My thought was that I would record interviews with high-performing people and talk to them about the extra ordinary lives that they were living.

Enter Jillian Sidoti. Jillian is an extra ordinary person who has done amazing things. I leave her story for her to tell, but I will say that I am constantly impressed by what she has done and is doing with her life. I met Jillian at a real estate conference in February 2019. Jillian was at the conference to present on the legality of raising private capital for real estate deals. After her talk, I walked up to her and asked her a few questions about the material she had presented. Since Brian and I were just getting into raising capital for our deals, I wanted to make sure I understood the subject as well as possible. While I was talking to her, I was wearing an *Old Fashioned Real Estate*™ shirt. She noticed the shirt and asked me about the show. She claimed that she was a fan and wanted to know when we would have her on the show. Her status as a fan is doubtful, because at the time we had only a few dozen subscribers and had released only about three episodes.

In truth, I was a bit starstruck. I knew who she was from her social media presence and also from her talk. The idea of having her on my show seemed farfetched. I pointed out to her that we didn't have guests on our show, and that since it was a drinking show and we filmed in Chattanooga, it would be difficult to have her come on. She offered to come to Chattanooga and sing the song "Chattanooga Choo Choo" on our show. Later that day, when I told Brian about her offer, I am fairly sure he didn't believe me. As it turned out, later that year, Jillian, Brian, and I were all scheduled to be at the same conference in Nashville, so we hatched a plan to record an episode with her. True to her word, Jillian even attempted to sing "Chattanooga Choo Choo" on the show. We had a great time, and we all ended up at an open bar party on Broad Street afterwards.

At that point, we still really didn't know each other, so we spent the time as most friendly strangers do, asking each other about our respective lives. It turned out that Jillian and I had a fair amount in common, with both of us being lawyers and growing up in the same era. However, since she was born in January 1978 and I wasn't born until April of that year, she is much older than me (put this in there for you, Jills). One of the things we talked about was about my idea for *Last Life Ever*. I had just started a Facebook group, bought the LastLifeEver.com domain, and had built my personal website with a bunch of references to *Last Life Ever*. I had even recorded a single episode of the show. What I think I told Jillian that day is that *Last Life Ever* is like a less gangster version of YOLO.

A few days later, I got a Facebook notification that Jillian Sidoti had commented on my post. I was excited; Jillian is a super-impressive person, and the idea that she knew who I was made me feel like I had really achieved something. Then I read what she wrote and went into a full panic. Jillian will tell you that I rarely, if ever, worry about anything, but this time I was worried. She had posted "Call me, I need to talk to you."

My brain immediately convinced me that Brian and I had done something wrong with our business and that we had violated some law. I was sure Jillian was going to tell me "You need to immediately fix this huge problem you created, and oh, you can't release the episode that I am on because I can't be associated with scumbags like you guys," or something like that. I didn't have her number, so calling her was possible. I sent her a PM that said "I don't have your number. Should I be worried? 'We need to talk' could be anything from ominous to 'I miss you.'"

Her response calmed me and to this day still amazes me: "No. No worry. I want to start a last life ever podcast with you."

That conversation took place in November 2019.

On March 16, 2020, we launched our show *Last Life Ever*. The show is a thousand times better with Jillian involved. She has pushed me to clarify our brand and our ideas. On the show we focus on three categories of people:

1. Extra ordinary people doing extra ordinary things
2. Ordinary people doing extra ordinary things
3. Ordinary people doing ordinary things that benefit us all

So far we have interviewed some amazing guests, including the youngest person to kayak the Zambezi River, an expert on sleep who shared with our listeners how to get better sleep, Olympic Gold medalists, famous authors, economists, comedians, and so many more amazing people.

If you haven't done so already, please check us out at LastLifeEver.com and subscribe to our show wherever you listen to podcasts. We also have an amazing private Facebook group, which you can find by searching "Last Life Ever" on Facebook or by going to https://www.facebook.com/groups/lastlifeever/.

I know I speak for Jillian as well when I say we look forward to getting to know you better.

Appendix B

LAW SCHOOL
GRADUATION SPEECH

I like to begin by offering, on behalf of the December 2006 graduating class, our sincere thanks to each of the people in this room. I doubt very much that there is anyone in this room that has not in some way contributed to our successes as we walk the final few steps in the long journey that brought each one of us to this point in our lives, to this great moment, to this wondrous occasion... Wow. If I am not careful this speech will turn into the average run-of-the-mill graduation speech and pretty soon everyone will be yawning, and then someone in the back of the room will start snoring and that will be that.

I think, instead I'd like, if it's okay with you, to offer a few brief thoughts about what it means to graduate with a juris doctorate degree.

Like many of the graduates here today, as a small child I had planned my life in advance, I knew what I wanted to be, I knew what I was going to do when I grew up. I was going to be the president, or maybe an astronaut, or a fireman, and if those things failed, I could always settle for becoming a lawyer. Well, I can tell you, right now, I have not settled.

There is no degree that I would rather be receiving, and there is no honor that I would rather have conferred upon me at this moment, than a juris doctorate from this school, from Michigan State University College of Law.

This degree that we receive today is a product of our lives. It's a product of our hard work and our endurance, an endurance inspired in no small part by our friend, the marathon runner. A few days ago, as I walked out of what should be the last exam of my academic career, I ran into that old friend, and I brought him here with me today. I did this because I believe that he still has something to offer us. This guy, this poster, has served to inspire us. It has instructed us to study long hours, to build our endurance so that when the time came, we could succeed. In asking us to remember the marathon runner, this poster has given us the model that has gotten us to this point. And over the next few weeks, as we prepare to take the bar exam, the training that we have done, the training that we have received here at this school, will make it possible for us to succeed.

Once we have taken and have passed the bar exam, and this guy's job is complete, I ask that you, the graduating class, in honor of this institution, and in honor of this poster remember the leprechaun.

You know, the one from the cereal box. The little guy who is always chasing after the pot of gold at the end of the rainbow. That leprechaun will, if you allow him to, offer you a chance to reflect, a chance to think about what it is that is important to you. You will be able to ask yourself, *Do I really want to work eighty or ninety hours a week, so that I can have my name on a door or a sign? What's really important to me? What do I really need from life?*

So ask yourself these questions, because right now as we receive this degree, and after we pass the bar exam, that rainbow of temptation will shine brighter than ever before. We will be able to catch glimmers of its golden treasure, and we will want to rush forward and grab that big pile of gold and take it for our own. But I caution you, and I caution myself, as that rainbow of opportunity grows ever brighter, to remember the leprechaun, because when it's all said and done, and when we finally arrive at the end of the rainbow, it sure would be a shame if all we found was a big bowl of cornflakes.

Thank you.

Appendix C

THE FOURTH OF JULY

When I was around fifteen years old, on July 5, some friends and I went to see the fireworks in Grandville, Michigan. That night I was inspired to write a poem.

Up in the sky great wonders unfold
Tales of men and women both young and old
Some came to see the majestical lights
And others came for social highlights

But no matter their reason
When it comes to this season
No one can deny
That they love the Fourth of July.

The Fourth of July is the first poem that I ever wrote on my own. It wasn't an assignment for a class, and there was no real reason for me to write it. I include it here because sometimes inspiration comes completely out of the blue. It only took me a few minutes to compose this poem, and I am under no illusion as to its quality. It's an okay poem, but not one of great importance to anyone other than me. The poem represents a distinct moment in my life. It is my sincere hope that you grab at those moments in your life and hang on to them. This poem is forever etched in my mind, and that moment when I first recited it to my friends always will be as well.

Appendix D
COMING SOON

I am nowhere near done with this life. I am constantly inspired by people around me. I often think about people like Arnold Schwarzenegger, who came from nowhere to be the best of the best—the best bodybuilder in the world, a huge action star, and ultimately governor of California. I am inspired by Buzz Aldrin, the second man to walk on the moon, who a few years ago traveled to the South Pole at eighty-eight years old. I am forty-four years old and healthier than I have been in years. I still have leukemia, and I am still over three hundred pounds, but I climbed to the highest point in Africa. I have a beach condo in Puerto Rico (full disclosure: I am renting for a year while I decide where I want to buy). I have a completed first draft of a science fiction novel that I am going to dig into and get ready to publish. My goals and aspirations are definitely different from yours—they are even different from my wife's. Becky is about to set out to hike the Appalachian Trail. Her thru-hike is scheduled to start March 8, and if all goes to plan, will be finished by mid-September 2022. When she finishes, she will have hiked more than 2,100 miles all the way from Georgia to Maine.

Every person has their own goals and their own dreams. However, sometimes these dreams overlap. Below, I share a few of the goals I set for myself recently in the hope that they will help inspire you to make big goals for yourself. I look forward to learning more about yours, and I hope that they likewise inspire me.

Jeff's Goals

1. Pray more and go to church regularly.
2. Never have bad days!
3. Stay alive: I want to keep living for as long as I can. This means I need to work out more and eat healthier (this is not a good goal because it's not quantified properly, but it's a core goal of mine, so I share it here).
4. Get below 278 pounds (this is the weight I weighed when I was married). I'd ultimately like to work my way down to below 250 pounds and stay there. I have unfortunately been stable around 320 to 325 pounds for nearly three years now, which is admittedly better than 420 pounds, but I want to make further course corrections.
5. 50/50/50/7 goal: visit fifty countries, fifty states, and seven continents before I turn fifty years old. I have

currently been to all fifty US states, thirty-nine countries, and all seven continents. I even made it to Antarctica during the pandemic.

6. Ownership in one thousand units of apartments.
7. Put together more and bigger deals for my investors.
8. Grow the *Old Fashioned Real Estate™ Show* from a thousand or so subscribers to ten thousand or more.
9. Launch and grow *Last Life Ever Podcast*.
10. Get this book published (presumably by the time you read this, I'll have this one done).
11. Rework science fiction book to ready for submission.
12. Climb Kilimanjaro (done—I did this in February 2020, just in time to avoid the global shutdown).
13. Take a zero-g flight.
14. Become a space tourist.
15. Buy an island house in a tropical climate (in process).
16. Have passive income sufficient to allow my wife to quit working and not have to worry about insurance benefits (done).
17. Increase income to $1 million per year.
18. Get a graduate certificate from Harvard (done).

This list is in no way complete and is not provided in any particular order. I have many more goals, some of which I choose to keep to myself, but many of which frankly would only bore or distract from the point. The point of course is to inspire. So go forth and reach for your goals.

Appendix E

TODAY IS A GOOD DAY!

"I never have bad days."
—Jeffrey Holst circa 1995 to present

The first draft of this book was completed in the middle part of the fall of 2019. I wrote 'these final thoughts' in April 2020:

The world has changed in dramatic and unforeseeable ways. I have chosen to preserve the bulk of the text without making substantial changes to the tone or the message. I am simply unable to foresee what is yet to come. Death rates from COVID-19 in the United States are continuing to climb, schools, businesses, and religious centers remain shuttered. Much of the rest of the world has it even worse. Today I spoke to a new friend, John. I met John in mid-February just after

I finished my Kilimanjaro climb. John is a Safari guide in Tanzania and guided a small group of us (including my wife, my brother, and his wife) into the Serengeti. The African trip was life-changing and eye-opening. It was not the first time I had seen real poverty, but it was the first time I slowed down amongst it and saw what it really was like to live in conditions that are so different from my own life. By Tanzanian standards, John is well off; he has a house and a small chicken farm. He has a good job and is well educated, but he is also suffering disproportionately to what we are experiencing. His elderly father is ill and lives three hours away by car. His town is locked down and the government is hinting at blackouts and water shortages. People are being forced to stay home, there is no money, there is no bailout, and there is no food. John is still better off than most. He has a gate around his property and they raise chickens.

There's a longer story here which I may someday tell, but when we were in Arusha, we lost our passports and ended up staying an extra day (they were eventually returned to us). During that extra day, after my brother and his wife flew to Zanzibar for some beach time, Becky and I hung out with John. We talked about starting a safari business together and we visited his home. As I write this today, that discussion was just a few weeks back—less than two months ago. The world is different now than it was then; the problems John and I discussed seem petty and insignificant now that so much has changed. Our future is less certain, and in the short term, John's future is bleak. People are starving and there is no way to get them food. Infection rates in Africa are skyrocketing and

I suspect that it's about to get very bad. Yet when I spoke to John about this, he told me that while it's very bad, he and his children still joke around and play. They have a running joke about what they are going to eat for dinner. Every day his kids ask him and he winks and says, "I feel like having chicken." John and his family are remarkable people. John was born into extreme poverty and has managed to secure a safe place for his family. In ordinary times they would be safe, secure, and well-fed, but now I worry for my extra ordinary friend. It is not an ordinary time and I do not have a crystal ball.

I don't know what the future will bring for us, for America, for Africa, or for the rest of the world but in truth, I am optimistic. This period of uncertainty is difficult, people are in pain, people are dying, but there are also signs of hope. Infection rates in Italy and Spain seem to be falling. People are self-isolating but also spending time videoconferencing with family and friends. The ultimate impact of this pandemic will not be known for years or even decades, but some things seem to be happening. People are taking their lives more seriously; they are being forced to recognize that time is fleeting and precious. People are taking stock of where they are in life and questioning how they can make it better. I firmly believe that there are people currently locked-up planning businesses, products, and innovations that will completely change the world. I don't know what those products or innovations will be, but I am excited to see what comes from this period. I could be wrong about the duration of the pandemic. I could be wrong that infection rates are starting to fall. This may be over when you read this or it may just be starting but it doesn't matter because today is a good day!

Go forth and embrace the world, do bigger and better things than you ever dreamed were possible. Expand your mind beyond your current confines. It doesn't matter if you are standing atop Kilimanjaro or locked in your basement waiting out a global pandemic. What matters is that you make the most of the time you have and that you reach for the life of your dreams.

"Today is a Good Day"

April 7, 2020
Chattanooga, Tennessee

FINAL THOUGHTS

Today really is a good day. Be blessed, live well. It's your last life ever—be sure to make it extra ordinary.

Jeff Holst
January 21, 2022

ACKNOWLEDGMENTS

So many people helped with the creation of this book that it would be nearly impossible for me to thank them all in this short section. That being said, there are a number of people that I absolutely have to acknowledge, because without their input, this would not be nearly what it is. The mistakes herein are mine alone, but the rest could not have existed without the following people.

My wife, Becky, to whom this book is dedicated. My mother, Janice Holst, who was my first editor. Jason and Karen Miller, who spent a huge amount of time reviewing and editing my drafts. Brian Levredge, who encouraged me to finish this book and who inspires me to be better at what I do. Travis Bronik, without whom I'd never had a chance to even consider writing this book. My coach and friend Dr. Jamil Sayegh. Father and Son, Tim and Adam Enochs, who introduced me to Morgan James Publishing and encouraged me to follow up and complete this process. All the amazing people at Morgan James. My numerous beta readers, including but not limited to my sister Kate H. Test, Jillian Sidoti, and Liz Hamby. My final editor, Lori Paximadis. The staff of the Track's End restaurant, including Autum, who put up with me, brought me coffee, and let me be as I wrote and rewrote sections of the book. And finally, all of the *Last Life Ever* community.

I am sure that I have forgotten more people than I recalled. Please don't feel left out—I swear I love you all.

ABOUT THE AUTHOR

Jeffrey Holst is a recovering attorney who hasn't had a bad day in more than a quarter of a century. Jeff pays for his love of adventure and travel through real estate investing. He has climbed to the highest point in Africa, swum with wild dolphins in the Red Sea, dodged sharks while diving at night in Australia, and hiked among seals and penguins in Antarctica. Jeff has been featured on hundreds of podcasts and radio shows, where he has shared his inspiring story of staying positive and overcoming adversity and achieving success despite multiple life-threatening illnesses and financial ruin. Jeff graduated early with honors from Michigan State University College of Law. He also holds an MBA. When they're not exploring the world, Jeff, his wife, Becky, and their Chihuahua, Trixie, split time between their homes in Chattanooga, Tennessee, and San Juan, Puerto Rico. Jeff is often referred to as the most interesting man in the world.

A free ebook edition is available with the purchase of this book.

To claim your free ebook edition:

1. Visit MorganJamesBOGO.com
2. Sign your name CLEARLY in the space
3. Complete the form and submit a photo of the entire copyright page
4. You or your friend can download the ebook to your preferred device

Morgan James BOGO™

A **FREE** ebook edition is available for you or a friend with the purchase of this print book.

CLEARLY SIGN YOUR NAME ABOVE

Instructions to claim your free ebook edition:
1. Visit MorganJamesBOGO.com
2. Sign your name CLEARLY in the space above
3. Complete the form and submit a photo of this entire page
4. You or your friend can download the ebook to your preferred device

Print & Digital Together Forever.

Snap a photo

Free ebook

Read anywhere

CPSIA information can be obtained
at www.ICGtesting.com
Printed in the USA
JSHW081558010523
41092JS00001B/70